Christian Marital
Counseling

Christian Marital Counseling

Eight Approaches to Helping Couples

Edited by
Everett L. Worthington Jr.

 BakerBooks

A Division of Baker Book House Co
Grand Rapids, Michigan 49516

Published by Baker Books,
a division of Baker Book House Company
P.O. Box 6287
Grand Rapids, Michigan 49516-6287

Printed in the United States of America

Library of Congress Cataloging-in-Publication Data

Christian marital counseling : eight approaches to helping couples / edited by Everett L. Worthington, Jr.
    p.   cm.
Includes bibliographical references and index.
ISBN 0-8010-5608-X
    1. Marriage counseling. 2. Marriage. 3. Marriage—Religious aspects—Christianity. 4. Church work with married people. I. Worthington, Everett L., 1946–
HQ10.C5 1996
362.82'86—dc20   96-9329

For information about academic books, resources for Christian leaders, and all new releases available from Baker Book House, visit our web site:
http://www.bakerbooks.com/

Contents

126531

Contributors

Dennis B. Guernsey, Ph.D., is professor of clinical family psychology and director of the graduate counseling programs at the School of Social and Behavioral Sciences at Seattle Pacific University, Seattle, Washington.

Willard F. Harley Jr., Ph.D., is a psychologist specializing in marriage and family therapy. He and his wife, Joyce, are the parents of two married children and have four grandchildren. Their home is in White Bear Lake, Minnesota.

Donald M. Joy, professor of human development at Asbury Theological Seminary, Wilmore, Kentucky, holds an M.A. in counseling from Southern Methodist University and a Ph.D. from Indiana University. Joy regards himself as an educator, not a therapist. He does premarriage and postmarriage consultation from a biblical, pastoral, structural-developmental theoretical base.

Savanna C. McCain, Ph.D., is a psychologist with Kaiser Permanente in Denver, Colorado. She has conducted outcome research on the effectiveness of PREP (Prevention and Relationship Enhancement Program), and has worked with the team at the University of Denver on PREP for a number of years. In addition to her contributions to Christian PREP, she has been working on the implementation of the program in local church settings.

Sherod Miller, Ph.D., is chairman of Interpersonal Communication Programs, a publishing and consulting company in Littleton, Colorado, specializing in communication skills training

7

and team building. He is codeveloper of the Couple Communication program.

Gary J. Oliver, Ph.D., is clinical director of Southwest Counseling Associates in Littleton, Colorado. He received his Th.M. from Fuller Theological Seminary and his doctorate in psychology from the University of Nebraska and has been a certified Couple Communication instructor since 1978. He also is currently a professor at Denver Seminary and program director for its marital and family therapy doctor of ministry program.

Les Parrott III, Ph.D., is associate professor of clinical psychology at Seattle Pacific University, Seattle, Washington. He is author of *Helping the Struggling Adolescent* and *Love's Unseen Enemy* and coauthor of *Saving Your Marriage Before It Starts* and *Becoming Soul Mates.* With his wife, he is codirector of the Center for Relationship Development at Seattle Pacific University.

Leslie Parrott, Ed.D., is a marriage and family therapist, the author of *The Career Counselor,* and the coauthor of *Saving Your Marriage Before It Starts* and *Becoming Soul Mates.* She and her husband direct the Center for Relationship Development at Seattle Pacific University.

Jennifer S. Ripley, B.S., is a graduate student in the counseling psychology program at Virginia Commonwealth University in Richmond. A graduate of Nyack College, she is focusing her research on marital dynamics and therapy.

Scott M. Stanley, Ph.D., is a psychologist, the codirector of the Center for Marital and Family Studies at the University of Denver, and an adjunct associate professor of marital therapy at Fuller Theological Seminary in Pasadena, California. He specializes in marital research and therapy.

Daniel W. Trathen, Ph.D., D.Min., is the program director of Southwest Counseling Associates in Littleton, Colorado. He is a visiting associate professor of marriage and family therapy and codirector of the doctor of ministry marriage and family therapy program at Denver Seminary.

Everett L. Worthington Jr., Ph.D., is a professor of psychology in the American Psychological Association-accredited counseling psychology program at Virginia Commonwealth University in Richmond.

H. Norman Wright is director of Christian Marriage Enrichment in Tustin, California. He is a marriage, family, and child counselor and former director of marriage, family, and child counseling at Biola University. He has written fifty-five books.

Preface

Marriage is held in highest esteem by Jesus as a metaphor for Israel's relationship with God, our spiritual relationship with Jesus, and the church's spiritual relationship with Jesus. The Christian community yearns to promote marital health through premarital education and marital enrichment and to heal fractured marriages (when fractures occur) through marital counseling. Over the years, compassionate, articulate, and loving Christian professionals have emerged, elaborating models for dealing with marriages. In presenting eight such approaches, this book is an easy-to-read resource for practicing therapists, pastors, graduate students in the helping professions, undergraduates interested in the practical integration of psychology and Christianity, trained Christian lay counselors, and lay people seeking an understanding of therapists' views of marriage and marriage counseling, who want to help others improve their marriages.

The basis for this book was a special issue of the *Journal of Psychology and Christianity* (vol. 13, no. 2), for which I served as issue editor. In order to provide a resource for those interested in Christian marital counseling, the leadership of the Christian Association for Psychological Studies (CAPS) has graciously granted permission to reprint the journal articles, which are supplemented in this book by responses to a case study of a fictitious couple (see the Introduction) and simulated dialogues between the therapists and the same couple.

The content of the Preface has been adapted from the Guest Editor's Page appearing in the *Journal of Psychology and Christianity* 13, no. 2:107.

In the journal articles, the authors summarized their theories of marriage counseling by responding to the same five questions—a format modeled on the 1980 special issue on psychotherapy in *Cognitive Theory and Research* (vol. 4, no. 3). Each of the eight approaches emerged in the authors' responses to these questions:

Question 1: What are the basics of your theory of marriage counseling? In your description, include your view of the typical cause(s) of marital problems and the typical goals of counseling.

Question 2: For what kind of people is your approach most appropriate?

Question 3: What are your foci for counseling?

Question 4: How is your marriage counseling conducted?

Question 5: How do you deal with a few of the common marital problems?

For this book, I gave the authors a description of a fictitious couple named Art and Pam and asked them to do two additional tasks:

Task 1: Respond to the case study by telling precisely how you might typically treat it, in how many sessions, in what order, and with what responses by the clients throughout counseling. One restriction: Assume that between the third and fourth counseling sessions with you—regardless of what had gone on during the previous session—the couple had a major argument and come to the fourth session in some crisis.

Task 2: Create a dialogue between the counselor and the couple (or one spouse, if you prefer) showing how you might deal with communication difficulties.

I gave the authors length restrictions for both the questions and the tasks.

The format was not intended to invite competitive comparison among the marital therapists or their theories, but to give a rounded sense of the wholeness of marriage, marital counseling, and marital psychoeducational interventions by allowing us to see the complementarity inherent across approaches. Now, as I see the entire book, I realize that there is enormous diversity in theories, approaches, and ways to express answers to the same questions. I realize, too, that there is much commonality among the therapists of various intellectual and theoretical persuasions, which affirms my belief that, despite substantial room for differences and individuality, there are more similarities than differences in approaches to and treatment of marital problems.

The contributors have affirmed the complexity of marriage as the intertwining of many different threads. And in turn, each author has woven a cloth with a few major colors. If we look at the whole, we see patterns shimmering with unique highlights, like Joseph's coat of many colors. Norm Wright and Les and Leslie Parrott have emphasized the crucial time of preparation for marriage—the couple when they are "green." Communication and conflict often deal with the "red" in marital relationships. Gary Oliver and Sherod Miller have stressed communication, and Scott Stanley, Dan Trathen, and Savanna McCain have emphasized conflict management. Bill Harley has paid special attention to romantic love—which could perhaps be thought of as the "hot pink" of marriage—and Don Joy has added other shades of "pink" by describing the sexual intimacy leading to pair bonding in marriage. Dennis Guernsey has emphasized the "royal purple" of the theological, with "unseen" insights from the psychodynamic unconscious. To strain the metaphor perhaps to (or beyond) the breaking point, I have provided the "white light" of an overall theme to unite various aspects of marriage—faith working through love.

Once you have read this volume, including the contributions of the collected authors and the final chapter evaluating the approaches, I hope you will have found it to be a valuable treasure in your library. I hope even more you will read and use this kaleidoscope often.

Introduction

A Case Study of Art and Pam

Presenting Problem

Art and Pam have sought counseling because they are extremely unhappy with their marriage. They have been bickering and arguing frequently, at times even yelling and cursing. They have general negative feelings toward each other and blame the other for the negative tone their marriage has taken in the last half year. Both Pam and Art are mildly depressed about the problem and feel that it is affecting their time away from each other as well as their marriage. They feel a loss of emotional intimacy and describe their feelings for each other as being "almost extinguished."

Relationship History

Art and Pam met sixteen years ago when both were seniors at a small Christian college in the Midwest. They dated throughout their last year of college and the year after they graduated. Finally marrying when both were twenty-four years old, Art and Pam have been married for fourteen years. (Both are now thirty-eight.)

After what Pam and Art admit was a rocky first year, things smoothed out in their marriage. Both worked—Art as an engineer and Pam as a manager-trainee in an advertising firm in St. Louis. They enjoyed becoming established as young professionals as well as being away from the small midwestern town where both sets of in-laws lived.

In Art and Pam's fifth year of marriage, several major changes occurred. Pam had a disagreement with her boss, who summarily fired her. Since a mild recession was underway, Pam could not find a new job, despite seeking employment for six months. At this time, Pam and Art decided to start a family. For almost a year, they tried to conceive, but were unable. Finally undergoing fertility testing, Art was discovered to be functionally sterile.

Shortly after receiving the test results, Art had a one-night, adulterous relationship with a coworker. Pam discovered the affair. Thereafter, Pam and Art had substantial conflict, went to marriage counseling with their pastor for eight weeks, and ultimately decided to move to a moderately sized city only thirty miles from both families of origin.

Both Pam and Art now claim that the affair has been forgiven and forgotten; however, several changes have become apparent in their relationship since Pam's discovery of the tryst. First, they have never felt as emotionally close as they once had. Second, their sexual life has been different, with Pam's reaching orgasm only about half the time because Art's manual stimulation is often "irritating." After the first year of marriage but prior to the affair, Pam had an orgasm virtually every time. Third, the two have begun to bicker and argue, which they had done only infrequently after their first year of marriage. Since the tryst, Art and Pam's relationship has not undergone any additional major crisis, but it has continued to deteriorate.

Families of Origin

Art is from a professional family of chemists. According to him, his mother and father's relationship is "spiritless." Art grew up as an only child, protected and mostly alone. He felt some emotional attachment to a favorite uncle and aunt, who much of the time were almost his surrogate parents, until their death when Art was in high school. Art originally aimed at being a scientist. As an adolescent, he rebelled and set his sights instead on being an engineer. "Some rebellion," he said with a self-critical sneer.

Pam is from a home of first-generation Italian-Americans. Both parents are emotionally expressive. Pam's mother did not work outside the home, but reared six children as "good Roman Catholics." Pam's father worked at a local grocery. The family had barely enough money to make ends meet. None of the children went to college except Pam, who entered a Protestant Christian college on a scholarship and worked her way through. In her junior year, she had a "conversion experience" at an Inter-Varsity Fellowship spring conference. Upset at Pam's leaving the Roman Catholic church, her parents broke off their relationship with Pam in an attempt to get her to come back to the church. When their rejection of Pam did not accomplish their desired goal, the parents eventually restored fellowship with her.

Art's parents did not seem affected when Art and Pam moved to St. Louis, but Pam's parents were angry. When Art and Pam moved back into the vicinity, Pam's parents began to visit or invite Art and Pam over to their house weekly. Pam's mother is especially critical of Art for not providing Pam with the emotional support she needs, though when Art and Pam visit, Pam's parents never voice their criticisms.

Individual Personalities

Art is a rational problem solver. Though capable of showing anger, he usually is indirect in its expression. He uses cutting criticism and put-down humor frequently and is sarcastic and openly critical of Pam.

Pam is very bright, verbally adept, persuasive, and vivacious. Although she is easy to like, Pam is a "manager." Almost everyone who meets her soon feels her directiveness. She generally expresses strong morals and is substantially more fundamentalistic in her Christianity than is Art, who is moral and conservatively Christian but more accepting of nonorthodox ideas.

Relationship Dynamics

Art and Pam exhibit a classic emotional distancer-pursuer relationship: Pam demands more closeness; Art demands more separateness. The more intimacy Pam demands, the more Art pulls away. However, during the few times that Pam has decided not to chase after Art, he has sought some limited contact.

Art and Pam say they used to talk about things that matter, but have become a couple who talk about daily business and not much else, unless they are fighting about something. They don't have many interests in common anymore. Pam likes to read—primarily Christian books and magazines—and Art likes to work at least four nights a week in a wood shop in their garage. Most other nights Art watches television. When Pam tries to watch with him, they end up sitting side by side until bedtime without talking very much.

Art says he hates to argue, but he still does it—often. Pam relates that she likes to talk things out, but she is frustrated because Art won't show any emotion except anger. They frequently interrupt each other and at times shout at each other simultaneously. Their arguments are loud and ugly.

Art and Pam blame each other for their marital problems. He blames her for being "pathologically controlling." She blames him for being self-centered. In one counseling session, Pam called Art "an egotistical, self-satisfied, nonexpressive lump who is more interested in himself and his own needs than in meeting any of my needs."

Pam and Art appear motivated to resolve their marital difficulties, both believing in the permanence of marriage as based on Scripture. Yet they cannot seem to break out of their mutually destructive patterns of behavior. Both acknowledge God's sovereignty and say they pray about their marriage problems, claiming they want God's will in their life and in their relationship.

Psychodynamic Marriage Counseling with Christians

Dennis B. Guernsey

Marriage counseling that is Christian begins with a counselor/therapist who is Christian. By this I mean that the integration of faith and therapy is primarily an issue having to do with the being and character of the therapist and client(s) rather than an identification of content or a platonic set of ideas. Only secondarily does it have to do with content (e.g., understanding and interpreting Scripture) or technique (e.g., quoting Scripture or praying during the session). For me, "Christian" as a word best modifies or describes a person or collective of persons who are followers of Christ. My suggestion is that the word *Christian* is somehow weakened when it is used to modify places or things, as in "Christian Yellow Pages," "a Christian resort and spa," or even "Christian counseling and therapy." The logical conclusion, if this is true, is that there is no such thing as "Christian marriage counseling" either as an idea or as a skill, only "Christian" people, "Christian" counselors, or "Christian" therapists.

Doing therapy is more of an art and less of a science (content) or technology (skills and technique). In the same way that no particular mode of doing art can or should claim to be Christian (e.g., realism, impressionism, expressionism, or cubism), no particular modality of therapy is particularly Christian. Whether one is cognitive-behavioral, existential, rational-emotive, or systemic is not the issue. What is the issue to me is the competency of the one who is doing the therapy. Is he or she good or skilled at doing therapy irrespective of the modality or orientation? More importantly, has Jesus Christ as Lord been integrated into the counselor's character, whatever his or her skill or competency level? Artists who are Christians do art; physicians who are Christians do medicine; scientists who are Christians do science; and sometimes Christians do marital therapy.

Question 1
What are the basics of your theory of marriage counseling? In your description, include your view of the typical cause(s) of marital problems and the typical goals of counseling.

A Theological Core

In the same way that I begin with Christ at the center of my life as a therapist, I begin with a theological core in my approach to doing counseling and therapy. The core I am suggesting is not peculiar to counseling and therapy. Rather, the issues are relevant to all of the human sciences.

Three essential theological issues form the core of my understanding and practice of counseling and therapy. They are an understanding of the doctrine of the *imago dei,* an understanding of the nature of sin and evil, and an understanding of the doctrine of covenant.

The imago dei. I begin with the anthropological concept of the *imago dei.* Specifically the work of Ray S. Anderson has been influential in my thinking. Anderson (1982) suggests that the core issue for any helping profession in terms of serving humankind is the doctrine of the *imago dei.* Human beings are created in the image of God and, thus, are to be accorded the highest regard and are to be treated with the utmost dignity. Whatever defaces that image is contrary to God's purposes for humankind. What we as therapists are about in terms of counseling and therapy is the influencing and treatment of the ones who reflect in their being the nature and character of God. Our work is serious business indeed. What counselors and therapists do is important both because of whom we serve (human beings and God) and because of whom our clients reflect (the living God).

A corollary issue in terms of a theological anthropology and one especially central to marriage counseling and therapy is the relational or social nature of the *imago dei.* When God created human beings in his image, the process involved the creation of a person in relationship with another person (Gen. 1:26–27). This social and relational nature of humankind is essential to what it means to be human. As such, the relational nature of human beings is at the heart of what we treat when we counsel. It is central even when we attend to individual psychotherapeutic issues. All counseling and therapy must at some time attend to the relational nature of the person or client. To ignore this relational core is to ignore our client's very nature. When we counsel men and women in their marriages, we are addressing the "and" in the equation "male *and* female" (Gen. 1:27, emphasis added; Anderson and Guernsey 1986; Guernsey 1982).

Sin and evil. In addition to the matter of a theological anthropology and the *imago dei* is an understanding of the human problem of sin and evil. I define sin as a disobedient missing of a mark, the falling short of the righteousness of God's glory (Rom. 3:23). We have all sinned and our world is marred by the consequences of our disobedience. Evil, on the other hand, is an act, whether deliberate or accidental, that leads to the defacement, degradation, or destruction of the *imago dei.* Evil and its consequences lie at the heart of most issues that compel a person to seek counseling or therapy. For example, in

21

the Old Testament, David's adulterous relationship with Bathsheba would be sin. His arranging for her husband's death was evil. Nathan's confrontation of David was for his evil actions (2 Sam. 11–12).

The significance of recognizing a distinction between sin and evil lies in the therapist's response to each. The therapist responds to sin by "holding" the client's story or disobedience, as described in D. W. Winnicott's (1988) description of the holding process in therapy, allowing the Holy Spirit to do the work of conviction (John 16:7–11). The therapist's response to evil is different, for it should be active, even confrontational if necessary. At this point, I agree with Scott Peck's discussion of the consequences of evil and its associated therapeutic imperatives (Peck 1978, 1983). Sin, though often tragic, is usually amenable to treatment and is open to love. Evil, even more tragic in terms of its consequences, resists treatment and will not be comforted by love.

Covenant. The third issue in this theological core is the scriptural teaching of covenant as I have discussed elsewhere (Guernsey 1984). Covenant has to do with promise making and promise keeping. In terms of counseling and therapy, I encourage my clients, especially those who are working through relational issues, to consider the promises they have made to one another as well as the promises they have broken. In my experience, they have typically broken more promises than they have kept, and the resulting sense of disappointment and disillusionment has overwhelmed their relationship. At this point, I seek to reframe their idea of promise or covenant. A quotation from *The Family Covenant* is appropriate:

> In the face of disappointment and habitual disillusionment, it is natural and understandable that we become disheartened. Even the best of us do. It's natural to have thoughts and fantasies of wanting out of the covenant, to be free of our promise. What is of greater importance is not the temptation to leave but the decision to hang in there. . . . (Guernsey 1984, 22)

My custom then is to describe the story mentioned in Exodus 32, a story of God's wanting to annul the covenant with Israel in the face of the people's disobedience and Moses' response to God's impulse. For those who are struggling with their relationships, especially in terms of the promises attendant to marriage, even the best of us sometimes want out of the promises we have made. Moses prevailed with God by reminding God of the promise to be and stay in covenant with Israel.

But what do you do when your spouse fails you as Israel failed God? The answer to this question forms, in my opinion, a radical approach to marriage. Again I offer my clients a quotation from *The Family Covenant,* "Implicit in every covenant is the certainty of betrayal. Embedded in every act of covenant-promise is the reality of disillusionment, disobedience and disheartenment" (Guernsey 1984, 22). My objective in this exchange with my clients is to reorient their idealism toward a more realistic perspective, a perspective that includes their struggle and failure as well as an orientation toward healing and forgiveness. Typically, at this point, an animated discussion takes place between the couple and myself having to do with their hurts, frustrations, and sorrows and with the subsequent need for them to show mercy toward one another, to forgive when and where needed, and to move on with the grace of God.

However, not all promises can and should be kept, especially when abuse and the degradation or the destruction of the *imago dei* are concerned. Not all marriages or relationships should be preserved. I remind the reader that Jesus said, "What therefore God has joined together, let not *man* put asunder" (Matt. 19:6 RSV, emphasis added). The implication of the verse is that God can annul what God has created. Based upon my understanding of the solemnity and importance of the *imago dei,* God always chooses the viability of the person and the dissolution of the institution if preserving the institution will result in the defacement or destruction of the person. The story of Jesus' dispute with the Pharisees over the Sabbath is an illustration of this principle (Mark 2:23–3:6). Jesus said that "the sabbath was made for man, not man for the sabbath; so the Son of man is lord even of the sabbath" (vv. 27–28 RSV). He then went on to heal a man with a withered hand *on the Sabbath.* That is, he set aside the institution of the Sabbath for the sake of the healing of the person. Sometimes, the same choices must be made regarding the protection of the person and the setting aside of the institutions of marriage and parenting. The preservation of the *imago dei* takes priority. Sometimes covenants must be set aside.

Psychodynamic Foundations

In terms of understanding marriages and the difficulties that are present in marriage counseling, my approach rests on three psychodynamic foundations: the attachment theories of John Bowlby (1969, 1973, 1980) and Mary Ainsworth, M. C. Blehar, and S. Wall (1978); the concepts of narcissism and narcissistic injury, as defined in the work of Neville Symington (1993); and the family-of-origin theories of Murray Bowen (1976) and Edward Friedman (1985).

Attachment theory. As defined by Bowlby, attachment theory suggests that the great issues of human experience revolve around the processes of early mother-child relationships involving attachment, subsequent issues of separation, and issues of unresolved loss and grief. These issues reflect the overarching rhythms of life. They are the relational specifics of the processes by which human beings become fully and competently human. They are the behavioral and affiliational blueprints of the *imago dei.*

Ainsworth followed Bowlby. Her early mother-infant research, performed first in Uganda in East Africa and subsequently at Johns Hopkins University, led to the identification of three significant attachment styles of mothering: secure, ambivalent, and avoidant. The secure relationship allows the child the freedom to be a child with the mother taking responsibility for the relationship. The positive consequences of this freedom are lifelong.

The ambivalent relationship involves the caregiver as being available at times and unavailable at others. The child becomes confused, falling prey to an intermittent pattern of chaotic presence. The child comes to believe that "sometimes she's here and it's great, and sometimes she's not, and it's terrible." This relationship yields the greatest degree of psychological disturbance in later life. The avoidant relationship involves a distancing between the mother and the child. If the mother is unavailable to the child, as would be the case of most neglect, the result is the child's inaccessibility to the mother. If the mother is "available" to the child but only as a means of meeting her own narcissistic needs, the child becomes distrustful and is, again, distant. According to attachment theory, much endogenous depression and emotional unavailability in adult life can be traced back to an avoidant attachment relationship with the earliest caregiver.

Each attachment style establishes an internal, relational templet upon which later, adult relationships will be forged. In terms of our discussion, the significance of early mother-infant attachment styles lies in the strong research verification that these relationships persist into adult life as parenting styles (Main and Cassidy 1988). Hence, it occurred to me in terms of my own academic research that perhaps attachment styles could be thought of as the architecture of subsequent adult relationships. It was a very short pschodynamic step that led me to explore the efficacy of attachment theory in predicting later marital choice and association.

Our research at Fuller Theological Seminary indicates that not only do attachment styles persist in adult parenting responses, they also persist in the choices and behaviors of couples in their marriages.[1] What this means in terms of my own understanding of counseling and therapy is that early mother-child relationships persist into adult life as factors in the relationships and in the marriages of the adult participants. Attachment theory can be used to explain adult behavior as well as to fashion our interventions in troubled marriages. The beauty of attachment theory is its jargon-free accessibility. Marriage counseling from this perspective involves the identification of early attachment styles and the recognition of their influences upon the present. Patterns of correction flow naturally from earlier patterns of attachment.

Narcissistic injury. The deliberate misparenting of children leads to their abuse and neglect, what Peck (1983) refers to as the parental origins of evil. As well, the more subtle abuse of unbridled child-

1. I refer here to research by Benjamin Wat, a marriage and family therapy doctoral graduate in the School of Psychology at Fuller Theological Seminary, Pasadena, Calif.

centeredness on the part of parents results in human beings who are bereft of relational skills. The abused and neglected child does not know how to bond, to communicate, or to solve problems. Yet, he or she mates and has children. This injury or woundedness of the child's soul results in what the British psychoanalyst Symington refers to as *narcissistic injury.* Interestingly, rather than speaking of mothers, Symington chooses to speak to the issue in terms of the "lifegiver." He asks,

> [W]hat is the person seeking later in life, in post-adolescence? If the direction is not to the self, what is it to? It is a mistake to say the infant is seeking the breast or the mother. . . . Instead, one has to posit the existence of an emotional object that is associated with the breast, associated with the mother, *or in later life associated with the other person.* It is in the other—an object that a person seeks as an alternative to seeking himself. . . . I call this object the "lifegiver." (1993, 35, emphasis added)

My suggestion is that the lifegiver is, in fact, the earliest attachment object, whether mother or father. According to Symington, the rejection of the lifegiver, whether for ambivalent or avoidant reasons in attachment terms, results in the child's selection of his or her own self as his or her love object. Thus, narcissism is the person's failure to bond with the lifegiver who is, in turn, the source of the *imago dei.* The lifegiver is the source of the person's human connectedness for good or for ill. The lifegiver is the one who is symbolically sought in later adult relationships. Most extramarital affairs, substance abuse, and kindred addictions can be explained as a pernicious quest for the lost lifegiver.

When the relationship with the lifegiver is secure (in Ainsworth's terms), subsequent adult relationships are likely to be secure. When the relationship with the lifegiver is ambivalent or avoidant, subsequent relationships are proportionately disturbed and dysfunctional. Others reap what we have sown, and the consequences of our lack of relatedness cascade to the next generation, and so on, and so on.

Family of origin. Bowen's family systems theory (1976) and its elaboration by Friedman (1985) form the last psychodynamic foundations of my understanding of counseling and therapy. According to Friedman, the family forms an emotional, intergenerational system whose strengths and weaknesses pass from one generation to the next (Friedman 1985). These intergenerational processes are projected by parents onto their children and are introjected by their children unconsciously. These generational patterns are ubiquitous, stubborn, and pervasive (see Guernsey and Guernsey 1990).

Friedman has stated that 70 percent of all presenting problems brought into therapy can be explained by intergenerational processes and introjects.[2] Family-of-origin issues, including a person's introjected parental marriage, are constantly at work in the present relationship. The past is never past and forgotten even though its memory in the present may be unconscious. What this means in terms of my theory of counseling and therapy is that generational issues, especially attachment patterns and narcissistic injury, must be uncovered and dealt with if there is any chance for change. These issues form the boundary conditions within which change occurs. They define the parameters of the therapeutic agenda.

Summary

In my theory of counseling and therapy, theological issues and psychological or psychodynamic issues are heads and tails of the same coin. I see them as interactive and complementary.

In terms of theological issues, an understanding and a valuing of the doctrine of the *imago dei* are necessary as it frames my ontological understanding of the human person. An understanding of the nature of sin and evil frames the substance of the problem and dilemma of being human. An understanding of the power of covenant defines the path of healing and restoration.

In terms of my psychology, attachment theory explains the psychodynamic core of what it means to be human. Narcissism and narcissistic injury define the dilemma of being human. And, the reso-

---

2. Edward Friedman, class lecture given at the School of Psychology, Fuller Theological Seminary, October 1989.

lution of family-of-origin issues defines the path or method of healing and restoration.

Question 2
For what kind of people is
your approach most appropriate?

I am stubborn and arrogant enough to believe that these core and foundational issues hold true for all humankind, irrespective of the viability of their faith commitments. When talking about them to people who are not Christians, I work at removing the God words, but I do not remove the fact that I am a follower of Christ. As far as I am concerned, the principles are still applicable. That is what clients get when they work with me. That is who I am. What is of interest to me is the heuristic value of the principles and the ease with which they can be explained.

Question 3
What are your foci for counseling?

I focus on the dynamics of the marital relationship as it is explained in terms of the earliest child-caregiver relationship and how those relationships are passed on through the generations. My relationship with my clients, in terms of the issues of transference, is one of a supportive coach. I am fairly active, inviting clients to take responsibility for themselves while at the same time inviting them to consider together with me their personal and generational stories.

In terms of emotion, behavior, and cognition, I tend to treat all of them with a somewhat modest disdain. That is, I believe the relational story of the person in terms of its generational and relational consequences lies at the center of the human dilemma. Feelings, doings, and thinkings are all important though secondary as compared to the essential properties of the client's story.

Question 4
How is your marriage counseling conducted?

Because I work from a modified family-systems perspective, the more folk I can get involved in the process, the better. I work hard at not becoming triangulated. If we are talking about a marriage, both partners need to be present. If we are talking about narcissistic injury, it is best if the respective caregiver(s) is present, though it is not necessary. At least, that is my goal. Even though we begin individually, we move to greater involvement of others as it becomes necessary and appropriate.

Question 5
How do you deal with
a few of the common marital problems?

The issue of divorce has been discussed earlier in this chapter (see pp. 22–24). Although I do not advocate divorce, I do encourage a person to consider it if the person's situation seems especially destructive. However, I work at keeping the choice as his or hers and not mine.

In terms of marital infidelity, I tend to focus on the need for each person in the marital dyad to connect with his or her "lost lifegiver" and the reality of the person's narcissistic injury. Somewhere toward the end of the process, I move toward encouraging the couple to extend mercy and forgiveness to one another. If they are Christians, I frame the issue in scriptural terms. If they are not, I use secular words. The need for grace, mercy, and peace does not go away simply because a person is not in the household of faith.

A therapeutic intervention possibly unique to me is my leading of the couple in a more realistic restatement of their wedding vows, usually toward the end of therapy. When the time comes for them to take this step, I try to make the occasion like their first wedding and as formal as possible, with witnesses and all. The heart of the ceremony is these words:

> I take you to be my lawfully wedded spouse with the full knowledge that you are weak as I am weak; that you will be unfaithful to me as I will be, if not in actuality, then in fantasy; that there will be times when you will disappoint me gravely as I will disappoint you. But in spite of this, I commit myself to love you, knowing your weaknesses and knowing the certainty of betrayal. (Guernsey 1984, 23)

Task 1
Respond to the case study by telling precisely how you might typically treat it, in how many sessions, in what order, and with what responses by the clients throughout counseling. One restriction: Assume that between the third and fourth counseling sessions with you—regardless of what had gone on during the previous session—the couple had a major argument and come to the fourth session in some crisis.

Most therapists who begin, as I do, with a basic psychodynamic assumption regarding their marriage counseling believe that when a couple walks down the aisle at their wedding, the two are never alone. My approach holds that significant others "walk down the aisle" with them in the form of internalized patterns of relationship, patterns that have a great deal of influence upon the course of the newly formed pair-bond.

Internalized patterns of relationship with significant others (i.e., the "family of origin"), if the patterns are hurtful and dysfunctional, often make a marriage more difficult and set the tone for conflict in the marriage for years to come. That is, an earlier narcissistic injury is relived time and time again. How does this happen? Perhaps a metaphor would be helpful, in this case the metaphor of a slide projector. I suggest that dysfunction in a marriage occurs when an earlier narcissistic injury, layered within the unconscious mind of the person, is projected onto the partner, much as the image of a slide in a slide projector is projected onto a screen. The image is really on the slide in the projector rather than on the screen, even though it appears otherwise. We can say that the image on the slide has been "transferred" onto the screen.

Early Narcissistic Injury

It is my belief that unresolved issues with our families of origin are projected upon those who become significant to us in the present—whether in our marriage, in our family of procreation (our relationships as parents with our children), or even in our work and career settings. Often, the issues are "inside" us rather than in the one onto whom we are projecting. However, when someone is in the midst of a fight with one's spouse, it is difficult, if not next to impossible, to believe that the whole of the problem is not the spouse's and the spouse's alone. Such is the nature of transference.

It is also my belief that the most significant issues we must deal with in terms of our families of origin, those that often lead to narcissistic injury, are the attachment patterns we had with our earliest caregivers. Research into early attachment between parents and children has been sorted into three patterns: secure, ambivalent, and avoidant attachment styles. Secure attachment relationships tend to lead to later-life secure relationships. The latter two attachment styles, which often lead to pain and conflict, are the ones related to Art and Pam's marital difficulties.

One of the most telling clues regarding early narcissistic injury is the communication penchant within a relationship characterized by a persistent cycle of blaming and defensiveness, a pattern that persists even when the content issues change. According to the case study, Art and Pam "have been bickering and arguing frequently. . . . They have general negative feelings toward each other and *blame* the other for the negative tone their marriage has taken . . ." (emphasis added). I understand the case as implying that this cycle has become ritualized. If the blaming/defensiveness cycle has been ritualized and is too persistent and if the couple is unable to step out of the pattern in my presence as a mutually supportive therapist, I will separate the couple in therapy, seeing them individually and working with them alone until they are able to resume therapy together. In Art and Pam's case, I assume they are able to suspend the blaming and defensiveness at least during our time together. Hence, I will work with them jointly.

Attachment Patterns

Art and Pam's case shows evidence of two family-of-origin attachment patterns that often lead to conflict in a marriage: an ambivalent attachment pattern between Pam and her parents and an avoidant attachment pattern between Art and his parents. My experience as a therapist suggests that the ambivalent/avoidant marital relationship is one of the most troubled of all the possible combinations of attachment patterns.

In terms of Pam, notice the push-and-pull emotional involvement between her and her parents. They are said to be "emotionally expressive," perhaps suggesting a kind of volatility in the home. When Pam left the Roman Catholic Church, "her parents broke off their relationship with Pam in an attempt to get her to come back to the church." It would be relatively safe to assume that such patterns of emotional cutoffs and their attendant turmoil did not begin with the conflict over religion. Indeed, they may have begun much earlier. I would explore at length these patterns with Pam, looking for previous instances of pushing and pulling, for other emotional cutoffs.

According to Art, his parents' marriage is "spiritless." The case indicates that Art "felt some emotional attachment to a favorite uncle and aunt, who . . . were almost his surrogate parents." Where were his parents? The case strongly suggests that they were missing and unavailable to Art; they just weren't there. Their abandonment, implicit in the case, probably began very early and would have been the source of much confusion, if not pain, in the young child. Such are the relational descriptors of an avoidant attachment pattern.

Especially significant in terms of Art and Pam's case is the fact that extramarital affairs are common in ambivalent/avoidant marital relationships, particularly on the part of the avoidant partner. Why? In the affair, the avoidant partner seeks a remedy for feelings of isolation. Sex is a great antidote for loneliness, and in an affair it comes without the demands of an ongoing, real-life, meaningful relational dialectic as would be the case in Art's marriage with Pam. An affair, though immoral, offers a too-easy fix for the avoidant spouse's existential longing.

Also significant is Pam's need to establish dominance in her relationships: She "is a 'manager'" and "almost everyone who meets her soon feels her *directiveness*" (emphasis added). From these words I infer a strong need for control on her part, a need to control that probably reaches into Pam's relationship with Art. Ambivalence in early childhood between a child and his or her primary caregiver(s) often leads to a need to control. An ambivalently attached child learns very early to seek control as a means of organizing his or her world in the face of the child's relationship with an ambivalent caregiver. Controlling others is the way the child learns to cope. (The ambivalent attachment pattern may also be the emotional root cause of most obsessive/compulsive behaviors, behaviors that can take the form of the need to control others in some marital and family conflict.)

The ambivalent/avoidant marital relationship is often characterized by distancing and pursuing. The ambivalent spouse (in this case, Pam) becomes the pursuer, repeating the earlier pursuit of the parent, and the avoidant spouse (in this case, Art) becomes the distancer, likewise acting out the child's defensive behavior, which is common between young children and their avoidant parents.

The Therapist's Role and Response to a Crisis

As a therapist, I attempt to establish with the couple an association resembling a secure relationship between a parent and a child without a sense of parental directiveness and authority. All therapy, in my opinion, involves a kind of reparenting. My role as the therapist, then, is to remain objective and supportive while containing the emotions and conflict of the couple. That is, I am to provide a secure environment. Hopefully, this safety will afford the partners the opportunity and the space to talk about their troubles. I try very hard not to take sides, often receiving the brunt of their anger (usually from the ambivalent spouse) because my objectivity is taken to mean that I do not care.

In the case of Art and Pam, they experience a crisis between the third and fourth therapeutic sessions. As an experienced therapist, I view this as progress and interpret it to them as such. Midstream crises in therapy are normal and sometimes occur because one or both partners need to curry favor with the therapist as a means of medicating their anxiety. Anxiety at this stage is predictable. I remind Pam and Art of their promises to one another (the language of covenant) and of the work they have agreed to do in therapy. I also suggest that the present conflict is inevitable given the transferences they are bringing to their marriage from their families of origin. What is more important in the long run is my ability as their therapist to stay objective and not to overreact. Pam and Art's crisis is paradoxical in the therapeutic setting, for they take the crisis to mean things are getting worse while I interpret it to mean things are getting better. Suggesting that there will probably be more crises, which will be normal and must be coped with one day at a time, I model for Art and Pam the attribute of security.

Not taking sides and forming a therapeutic alliance *with the couple* allows me to empathize with Art and Pam's pain and to be an advocate for their marriage, that is, the covenant between them. Such a stance also allows me to point out, when appropriate, the positives and possibilities in their marriage, characteristics that are easily overshadowed by their troubles. Because Pam and Art are Christians, I use the language of Scripture: covenant, forgiveness, mercy, and "speaking the truth in love" (Eph. 4:15 RSV). I talk freely of God's love and available grace. For me, this is not rhetoric. God's love and grace are fact, and they are powerful.

In the course of the therapy, and without necessarily labeling it as such, I interpret Art and Pam's conflicts in terms of their attachment patterns and the transferences they are making in their marriage. Gradually, Art and Pam begin to see the connections, too. Over a period of time, my secure relationship with their marriage coupled with a steady opportunity to talk objectively about family-of-origin issues allows for a special kind of healing to take place.

The miracle is that given time the wholeness of Pam and Art's relationship will emerge and prevail. I believe that because they are created in the image of God, their relationship contains a de facto capacity for wholeness. The concept of the *imago dei* is a relational phenomenon applicable within a person and between persons. This relational nature of the *imago dei* holds true for those outside the body of Christ as well as those within. Indeed, it forms the basis of the work we do with those outside the church. Art and Pam's saving relationship with Jesus Christ assures me that the Spirit of God will be accessible to them and will be a comforting and natural resource. Under normal conditions, I would expect therapy with the couple to extend from four to six months and to end positively.

Task 2
Create a dialogue between the counselor and the couple (or one spouse, if you prefer) showing how you might deal with communication difficulties.

My experience of thirty years as a therapist has shown that I need to make myself "small" in order for the couples to grow "bigger." By *small* I mean what Bowen refers to as "not knowing." The idea is for me to get progressively smaller while staying present and involved. This approach is especially appropriate when the issue is communication, as one such issue is in the case of Art and Pam. Couples *want* to communicate, even to the point of communicating dysfunctionally. Since they cannot *not* communicate, the key is to provide a vehicle or a device for them to use that will increase the level of their positive communication while at the same time decreasing the level of their negative or destructive habits.

One process I use to promote better communication is the "marriage conference," which Ray Corsini of the University of Hawaii introduced to me. The marriage conference is especially useful with severely conflicted couples as a means of building a sense of good will between the partners. I would use this device with Art and Pam by giving them the instructions that follow.

Marriage Conference Instructions

1. Choose a time when you both are relatively rested and when you will absolutely not be interrupted.
2. Place two kitchen or dining-room chairs back-to-back.
3. Take one timer from the kitchen and set it for five minutes.
4. Sit in the chairs, facing in opposite directions. One of you should begin talking and continue for five minutes. (What you talk about is totally up to you; you can talk about yourself, your marriage, current events, or anything else. The person talking determines the content of the speech.)
5. The person talking is not to be interrupted. The other party is to listen.
6. When the timer rings, reset it for five minutes. The other person is now to begin talking. The same conditions apply: The person talking is not to be interrupted, and the other party is to listen.
7. When the timer rings for the second time, reset it for another five minutes. The person who talked first talks for this second turn.
8. When the timer rings, stand up and go your separate ways with absolutely no contact for one hour. (After that one hour, life can return to normal.)
9. At least twenty-four hours later, have another conference with the same restrictions and conditions.
10. This time, however, reverse the order of talking. That is, the person who previously went second now goes first and third, and the person who previously went first now goes second, talking only once.

11. Observe the one-hour break after the conference.
12. Be prepared to talk about your experience the next time we meet.

The marriage conference is a behavioral device that places boundaries and time-specific parameters around what so easily becomes the interminable, downward-spiraling process so common in highly conflicted couples. This vehicle removes most of the nonverbal communication between partners, requires each partner both to talk and to listen, and requires the partners to take turns. Extremely useful as a snapshot of the relationship, the marriage conference aids the therapist in learning a great deal about the couple's communication patterns in their report during the next session, especially if they failed to complete the assignment or if one partner sabotaged the process. When a couple is unable to complete the task after two tries, it probably means they will be unable to work in therapy as a couple and, instead, need to be seen individually. However, many couples experience the process as hopeful.

It may seem paradoxical that a therapist who relies so heavily on psychodynamic processes in his work depends on a behavioral device when teaching about communication. Though I do lean on psychodynamics, I am also a pragmatist, who is more concerned with what works than I am with an idea and with theory. In terms of teaching about communication, the marriage conference seems to work better than most other devices.

References

Ainsworth, M., M. C. Blehar, and S. Wall. 1978. *Patterns of attachment.* New York: Lawrence Erlbaum Associates.

Anderson, R. S. 1982. *On being human.* Grand Rapids: Eerdmans.

Anderson, R. S., and D. B. Guernsey. 1986. *On being family.* Grand Rapids: Eerdmans.

Bowen, M. 1976. *Family therapy in clinical practice.* New York: Brunner/Mazel.

Bowlby, J. 1969. *Attachment.* New York: Basic Books.

———. 1973. *Separation.* New York: Basic Books.

———. 1980. *Loss.* New York: Basic Books.

Friedman, E. H. 1985. *Generation to generation: Family process in church and synagogue.* New York: Guilford.

Guernsey, D. B. 1982. *A new design for family ministry.* Elgin, Ill.: David C. Cook.

———. 1984. *The family covenant.* Elgin, Ill.: David C. Cook.

Guernsey, D. B., and L. Guernsey. 1990. *Birthmarks: Breaking free from the destructive imprints of your family history.* Waco, Tex.: Word Books.

Main, M., and J. Cassidy. 1988. Predicting rejection of her infant from mother's representation of her own experience: Implications for the abused-abusing intergenerational cycle. *Child Abuse and Neglect* 8:203–17.

Peck, M. S. 1978. *The road less traveled.* New York: Simon and Schuster.

———. 1983. *People of the lie.* New York: Simon and Schuster.

Symington, N. 1993. *Narcissism: A new theory.* London: Karnac Books.

Winnicott, D. W. 1988. *Human nature.* New York: Schocken Books.

Teaching Couples to Fall in Love

Willard F. Harley Jr.

What career would you choose if you were financially independent? That was the question my father asked me when we first discussed my career alternatives. His point was that I should choose a career, not depending on how much money I would earn, but rather on my passion for the field itself. So I graduated from Westmont College in Santa Barbara in 1962 with a major in philosophy and no idea how I would earn a living.

With "passion for the field" as my guide, I then attended the University of California-Santa Barbara for two years as a limited graduate student, taking courses in a wide variety of majors. During that time, I married the love of my life, Joyce, who gave birth to our first child, Jennifer. My father-in-law must have been horrified by my lack of progress toward a career that could support his daughter and grandchild. It was time for me to be reminded that I was not financially independent! I had to get a paying job soon. So I chose a career in psychology, earned a Ph.D. degree by 1967, and found my first job teaching psychology at the University of California at Riverside.

My father, also a psychologist, had earned a living teaching psychology. But in his spare time he was also a marriage counselor. He earned little or nothing for his counseling services, considering it to be a Christian ministry. His approach was biblically based, and in the process of restoring marriages, he led many of his clients to the Lord. His counseling sessions were often Bible studies.

I also counseled couples in my spare time, starting at the age of nineteen. I charged nothing for my services, and it did not occur to me that anyone could, or should, make a living at it. If a couple would ask my advice, I would try to help them using the same biblically based approach of my father. I was not very successful, but couples continued to seek my help.

There were many ways to explain my failure. I felt, at first, that it was my youth, that I was too young to influence couples to do what I suggested. Furthermore, I was not as experienced in using Scripture as my father had been. But when I discussed with my father counseling techniques and his recent cases, I became aware that his methods were not as successful for him as they had been in the past. Changes were taking place in marriage in particular, and our society in general, that were making traditional approaches to Christian marriage counseling ineffective.

There had been no divorces in my family for generations, and I had assumed that once you married someone, it was for life. I was raised with a belief in unconditional commitment. In other words, regardless of my spouse's behavior, I should try to love her and be a good husband as my service to the Lord. And yet, my experience with Christian couples led me to the conclusion that my beliefs were in the minority. Most couples I saw seemed to have a total lack of commitment to marriage.

What I did not understand then was that the tremendous social change taking place in our society would rip apart Christian and non-Christian marriages and families for decades to come. And schools that taught future marriage counselors reflected the change in moral values. Rather than teaching unconditional commitment to marriage, they taught that marriage was often a trap that prevented individuals from achieving their potential. It contributed mightily to an unprecedented wave of broken homes. If I were serious about helping couples in today's marriages, I would need to understand the values of our society and what they were doing to our marriages. Saving marriages became an interest that consumed much of my time and attention.

Question 1
What are the basics of your theory of marriage counseling? In your description, include your view of the typical cause(s) of marital problems and the typical goals of counseling.

My effort to create an effective approach to marriage counseling began in 1973. I was teaching psychology at Bethel College in Saint Paul, Minnesota, and my private counseling was taking almost all of my spare time. (I was still not charging a fee, which probably explained much of my popularity.) My failure to help couples overcome marital problems finally drove me to change my counseling approach.

Up to that point, the theory I had been using was biblically based and well reasoned: When a couple agreed to marry each other, they made a commitment to God. They promised before God and witnesses to love and care for each other until they died. My job as a counselor had been to remind them of that promise and encourage them to follow God's will for their lives. It did not work! I had been assuming that Christians would seek God's will. Perhaps these couples were not Christians, I reasoned. Perhaps one was a Christian but the other was not. Maybe they did not care what God thought. Whatever the answer, I was faced with the fact that Christian marriages were failing in unprecedented numbers.

Couples were telling me that they did not *want* to care for each other anymore. They wanted someone to care for them, but also

41

wanted to be free to pursue their own interests even if it was at the expense of their spouses. The ever increasing self-centeredness and thoughtlessness that were permeating our society were permeating the lives of Christians as well. Christians were not only willing to disobey God, but also willing to watch their children suffer. I came face-to-face with the fact that in our society, even among Christians, a genuine commitment to lifelong marriage had been replaced by a commitment to personal ambition. Those who dedicated their lives to their spouse and family were regarded as naive at best and as victimized at worst.

After failing to save marriages by trying to impose my values on couples, I finally came to the point where I asked *them* what would work. What could I offer them to save their marriage? They gave me the answer.

I had been resisting the obvious: In our society, people marry because they love each other, and they divorce because they lose that love. Romantic love drives most marriages, and without it most couples will abandon their beliefs and their children to escape a love-less relationship. What they want is romantic love, and they want it at all costs.

As I struggled with these observations, I remembered the insights of Leon Festinger (1957), who argued that we try very hard to reduce conflicts within ourselves, which he called *cognitive dissonance*. When our emotional reactions and behavior are in conflict with our attitudes and beliefs, we are very unhappy. Since it is apparently easier to change attitudes and beliefs than it is to change emotional reactions and habits, we tend to create new attitudes and beliefs that provide justification for those reactions and habits.

These insights help explain how a pastor can tell me with all sincerity that he believes it is God's will for him to divorce his wife so that he can find sexual fulfillment with his church secretary. After all, he rationalizes, God is love and has obviously approved of the secretary since they love each other so much. He wants to continue in his ministry and cannot understand why the church would want him to leave.

The truth is that the pastor is out of God's will, but he tries to convince himself, and me, otherwise. Why does he do it? To minimize the conflict within himself. The rationale works for him and that is what counts. You can see his error because you are not the one having the affair. If pastors and Christian leaders find justification for divorce when their emotions no longer support their commitment to marriage, it is easy to see how most other couples, whether Christian or not, find such justification, too.

With all this overwhelming evidence, I began to recognize the importance of attacking emotions rather than commitment. When one or both members of a couple are no longer in love, the marriage is in danger of dissolution. If romantic love is restored, the danger passes. There is no need to even mention commitment, since it will naturally follow, as Festinger would predict.

Why is it so easy for couples to commit themselves to lifelong marriage at the wedding? Because they are both in love with each other. The true test of commitment comes when love is lost, and I have seen most couples fail that test in our present-day society.

Today, the most important reason we marry is that we are in love. I rarely find individuals who shunned the one they loved to marry someone they did not love. Marriage without romantic love makes no sense to most people in the United States. And it is easy to commit yourself to one you love because you do not expect the feeling to leave. You expect to be in love with that person the rest of your life. But when the feeling of romantic love, that feeling of incredible emotional attraction, disappears, most people feel that they made a terrible mistake to have ever married that person. And they cannot bear the thought of a lifelong relationship with someone they do not love.

What causes people to marry each other in our society? It is romantic love. What causes people to divorce each other in our society? It is the loss of romantic love. It is that simple. With these insights I had gained by 1973, I set out to achieve a new goal in marriage counseling: Help couples re-create the experience of romantic love. To make the goal easier to understand, I created the concept of the "love bank."

43

We all have a love bank, and those we know have accounts in it. When people do things that make us feel good, "love units" are deposited, and when they do things that make us feel bad, love units are withdrawn. When couples meet each other's most important emotional needs, so many love units are deposited that they experience romantic love. So the goal of marital therapy is to help couples deposit love units by meeting each other's most important emotional needs. Once that is achieved, they are in love with each other and the risk of divorce is ended.

My concept of the love bank, and romantic love itself, comes from a particular brand of neobehaviorism that I find appealing. The theory is that if a positive emotional reaction (feeling good) is associated with a particular object (your spouse) often enough, exposure to the object will eventually elicit the positive emotional reaction all by itself. It is called conditioning. In the same way, when a negative reaction is repeatedly associated with an object, the object will produce a negative reaction. I expanded on the concept to help people realize that when they make each other feel good, they will find each other's very presence to be attractive. And when they make each other feel bad, each other's presence will be repulsive. When they meet someone's most important emotional needs, so many love units are deposited that the phenomenon we call romantic love is experienced. It is in the very best interest of a married couple to try to make each other feel good and avoid making each other feel bad.

When we stop to think about it, is not this what Christ said all along? Not in so many words, of course, but he certainly did want us to make others feel good, particularly the one we marry, by meeting their needs. And in his Sermon on the Mount (Matt. 5–7), Jesus encouraged his followers to avoid making people feel bad, even if they tried to make his followers feel bad. As applied to marriage, we are not to be the cause of our spouse's unhappiness, even if we think he or she has become our enemy. Christ wants us to be the cause of our spouse's happiness, and he wants us to avoid being the cause of his or her unhappiness. When Christ's teachings are followed in marriage, romantic love is the result.

I began to use a form of transaction, or exchange, theory to motivate couples to restore romantic love. My argument was as follows: (a) If you were both in love with each other, you would be happy with your marriage and the threat of divorce and a broken family would end; (b) romantic love is created when you make each other feel good; (c) you make each other feel good when you meet each other's most important emotional needs; therefore, (d) learn to meet each other's most important emotional needs, and you will restore romantic love to your marriage. To get the ball rolling, I encouraged a couple to dedicate three months to becoming an expert at meeting each other's *most* important emotional need.

The exchange, or transaction, is this: If you meet my most important emotional need, I will meet yours. This is not an unconditional commitment, it is a *conditional* commitment—and only for a limited period of time. But at least it was something that couples were willing to do. I saw the partners individually to discover their emotional needs and then worked with them individually to teach them how to meet each other's most important needs. If each one's most important emotional needs were met, the two should eventually be in love with each other.

When I first started negotiating exchanges, I found that, in general, men wanted more and better sex and women wanted more and better affection, conversation, or both. In learning how to help couples improve their sexual relationship, I was greatly influenced by Helen Singer Kaplan (1974). Men were particularly impressed with my approach and its effectiveness, and their wives were happy to have found a counselor that their husbands would respect. With the promise of more and better sex, men were motivated to become more affectionate or conversational. Once progress was made with each spouse's most important emotional need, we would go on to other emotional needs. The strategy was on target for so many couples that I became known as the "miracle worker."

By discussing emotional needs privately with hundreds of men and women, I discovered that almost everyone expressed the same ten emotional needs (sexual fulfillment, affection, recreational companionship, conversation, physical attractiveness, financial support, domestic support, honesty and openness, admiration, and family commitment). But I also discovered that men and women tended to list these needs with an entirely different priority. The five *most* important emotional needs of men were the *least* important for women, and vice versa. What an insight! No wonder men and women have so much difficulty meeting each other's needs: they lacked empathy. They did for each other what they would appreciate the most, but it turned out that their efforts were misdirected. What they appreciated the most, their spouses appreciated the least!

Question 2
For what kind of people is your approach most appropriate?

When my success rate climbed to over 90 percent in 1977, I resigned from my teaching position to counsel full-time. Over a period of ten years, my solo practice developed into thirty-two separate locations with over one hundred counselors. I trained the counselors myself and branched out into chemical-dependency treatment as well as family therapy. I also provided training to over one hundred Minnesota pastors.

My approach to marriage counseling has worked well in both rural and urban communities, across racial boundaries, with a broad age spectrum, for many religious orientations, and for those with no religious interest at all. It seems to get to the very core of what marriages are all about. The methods I use are helpful to both Christian and non-Christian clients. While I feel that the values are based on Scripture, a couple need not believe the values to benefit from the methods. The success of the methods often helps change their values. The goal of therapy is to restore romantic love to marriage, and both Christians and non-Christians share a willingness to achieve that objective.

Question 3
What are your foci for counseling?

In 1986 I wrote my first book on marriage counseling, *His Needs, Her Needs*. I wrote it primarily as a text to give the thousands of clients that we served each year, never expecting it to be popular beyond my network of clinics. (Much to my surprise and delight, it has become increasingly popular, with sales increasing each year since it was published.)

If couples are to build romantic love, they must meet each other's most important emotional needs. But that is only half the story. Couples that deposit love units can also withdraw love units. To protect romantic love in marriage, a counselor must not only teach couples how to deposit love units, but also how to avoid withdrawing them! With that purpose in mind, I wrote *Love Busters* (1992).

A "love buster" is a habit of one spouse that causes the other to be unhappy. Since it withdraws love units from the love bank, it is a love buster. I divide common love busters into five categories: (a) angry outbursts, (b) disrespectful judgments, (c) annoying behavior, (d) selfish demands, and (e) dishonesty. Couples who read *Love Busters* are encouraged to overcome these destructive habits to protect the romantic love they have for each other.

I help couples understand how to avoid love busters with my "policy of joint agreement": Never do anything without the enthusiastic between agreement of you and your spouse. This rule helps couples learn how to become thoughtful and sensitive to each other's feelings. If partners follow this policy, they avoid countless love busters because no one will enthusiastically agree to something that hurts the other. That is, the policy creates the opportunity to restore romantic love by making marriages safe.

My policy of joint agreement is antithetical to the philosophy of our society—do whatever makes *you* happy. The policy makes couples consider each other's happiness as equally important. But why would partners agree to it when they have been taught all their lives to do the opposite? Because the hope for romantic love is so strong that the policy that helps create it is given serious consideration, even in our society. Once the policy of joint agreement is accepted by a couple, it helps insulate them from many of the destructive forces that are ruining marriages.

Question 4
How is your marriage counseling conducted?

In both of my books, I refer to forms that I use in marriage counseling. But because of space limitations and the size of the books, it was impractical for most of the forms to be printed. So I wrote the workbook *Five Steps to Romantic Love* (1993), which contains most of the forms I created to help couples identify their marital problems and to document the way they should go about solving them. While this workbook is essentially a companion text for the readers of *His Needs, Her Needs* and *Love Busters,* it is also a summary of the latest version of my marital theory and how I conduct marriage counseling. It begins with a revision of a concept that I abandoned in 1973—commitment.

The *first step to romantic love* is signing an agreement that commits a husband and wife to (a) avoid being the cause of each other's unhappiness (love busters), (b) meet each other's most important emotional need, and (c) spend fifteen hours every week giving each other undivided attention. It is a commitment to the process of restoring and guarding romantic love. When that goal is achieved, the commitment to remain married and in love until death, which I wholeheartedly support, does not even need to be mentioned.

The *second step to romantic love* is identifying the love busters in marriage. Forms are printed for both husband and wife to complete that identify and prioritize the habits that create pain or discomfort in marriage. The *third step* is overcoming the love busters that were identified in the second step.

The *fourth step to romantic love* is identifying each spouse's five most important emotional needs, and the *fifth step* is learning to meet those needs. The entire program is designed to help couples eliminate the withdrawal of love units and learn to deposit them in each other's love bank. By so doing, they create and sustain romantic love, which also preserves the security of their marriages and families.

One form that I have found very useful, but have not printed in its entirety, is my Love Bank Inventory (see Additional Resources on p. 61). It is a twenty-item questionnaire that measures romantic love. I use it when I counsel couples to help me know whether progress is being made. A ten-item version of this questionnaire is printed on the back cover of *Love Busters,* and you are welcome to use it as you counsel couples.

My approach to marital therapy is ready-made for counselors with a cognitive-behavioral background. I emphasize the role of marital beliefs and values that appeals to those with a cognitive orientation, and I also focus on the role of marital habits that behaviorists understand and appreciate. Since I begin with a goal, romantic love, use various methods to achieve it, and measure success or failure in reaching it, I clearly fall into the category of directive therapy.

Question 5
How do you deal with a few of the common marital problems?

My marital theory can be adapted to many formats: marital therapy, marital enrichment, or premarital counseling. Since the creation and maintenance of romantic love is of interest to just about anybody who is married or plans to be married, the methods I use can be introduced whenever the subject of marriage is the focus of attention. However, each format demands a certain emphasis.

Marital therapy usually finds couples out of love and contemplating divorce. An emphasis on love busters and how they create emotional conflict and withdrawal helps couples understand why they feel the way they do. It also helps them plan a marital reconciliation that begins by eliminating destructive marital habits rather than rushing into the task of meeting emotional needs. When a husband and wife are emotionally withdrawn from each other, they do not want their needs met by their spouse. It is only when they feel safe enough to lower their defenses that the meeting of emotional needs is possible. It is at that point that marital therapy can provide training in meeting important emotional needs.

A marital enrichment format, by contrast, can emphasize ways to meet a spouse's most important emotional needs right from the beginning. Those who attend marriage enrichment seminars should have overcome love busters and should be wanting to create a deeper, more caring relationship. By the way, when those who have not overcome love busters attend these seminars, they often open such a can of worms that couples leave in worse shape than when they came. I believe that couples in a state of emotional withdrawal or emotional conflict should be in marital therapy, not marital enrichment seminars.

In a premarital counseling format, a counselor would educate a couple in each area of marital commitment emphasized by my theory: (a) learning to avoid being the cause of each other's pain and discomfort by protecting each other from love busters, (b) learning to meet each other's most important emotional needs, and (c) giving each other undivided attention a minimum of fifteen hours each week. My Agreement to Overcome Love Busters and Meet the Most Important Emotional Needs found in *Five Steps to Romantic Love* would be carefully read, discussed, and finally signed by an engaged couple.

The last chapter in *Five Steps to Romantic Love* is entitled "How to Find a Good Marriage Counselor." It serves as a guide to couples who need counseling, but do not know what to expect or what to look for in a counselor. It also provides insight into my personal biases. What I recommend in a marriage counselor is what I have tried to do myself.

The chapter begins with a statement of the purpose of a marriage counselor. I explain that he or she should be able to guide a couple through (a) emotional minefields, (b) motivational swamps, and (c) creative wildernesses.

Emotional minefields are the overwhelmingly painful experiences of couples when they try to adjust to each other's emotional reac-

50

tions. Hurt feelings, depression, anger, panic, and paranoia are just a few of the land mines that pop up without warning. A good marriage counselor should help couples avoid these land mines and provide effective damage control when they explode unexpectedly.

Motivational swamps are the feelings of discouragement couples may feel while working toward marital reconciliation. My experience with clients is that they are poorly motivated to do what is necessary to create romantic love. A good counselor helps provide the inspiration necessary to get the job done.

Creative wildernesses are the characteristic inabilities of couples in marital crisis to discover solutions to their problems. An otherwise creative couple becomes slow-witted when faced with marital disaster, and a good marriage counselor can often be their only source of an effective strategy. He or she can also help restore their creativity by drawing out their intelligence from overlays of emotion.

Once I describe the purpose of a marriage counselor, I go on to explain how to make the first appointment, what the cost should be, what to expect in the intake session, what to expect in the assessment session, and what to expect during treatment. This description closely follows the procedure that I have used in my counseling practice.

Task 1
Respond to the case study by telling precisely how you might typically treat it, in how many sessions, in what order, and with what responses by the clients throughout counseling. One restriction: Assume that between the third and fourth counseling sessions with you— regardless of what had gone on during the previous session—the couple had a major argument and come to the fourth session in some crisis.

To help me describe my counseling procedures, I will create a fictionalized account of how I would treat the reference case study of

Art and Pam. They do, however, represent other, similar couples whom I have treated, and so my account reflects a fairly realistic description of my approach to the problem and a typical outcome. I will describe the conflict mentioned in the task statement in the next section.

Prior to their first appointment, Art and Pam were given an opportunity to talk to me on the telephone. This helped them decide whether or not my counseling style would be comfortable for them. There was no charge for this brief conversation. When they decided to use my services, I encouraged them to begin therapy within a day of their decision. Motivation for marital counseling is usually very low, so I did not want them to have time to change their minds.

The first (intake) session gave Art and Pam a chance to explain to me their perspectives of the problem. They did this individually so that they could be honest with me and not fear retaliation when they returned home. At the end of this session, I brought them together to ask them to complete several questionnaires: (a) the Minnesota Multiphasic Personality Inventory (MMPI), (b) a personal history questionnaire, (c) the Emotional Needs Questionnaire, (d) the Love Busters Questionnaire, and (e) the Love Bank Inventory.

I gave them a short pep talk, explaining that these questionnaires would be the most difficult part of the entire therapy, and once they were completed we could get to work on improving their marriage. I instructed them not to share the results with each other and warned them not to discuss anything that might cause a fight. I completed the intake with an appointment for the assessment session, which I made personally.

The assessment session was scheduled for a week later. Sometimes I encourage couples to see me within a few days since I do not want them to lose their motivation before we have had a chance to make any changes in the way they treat each other. But I judged Art and Pam to be stable enough to wait a week. As during the intake, I saw Art and Pam separately for the assessment. Although I looked into their backgrounds, the information was not too helpful except that it prepared me for their "explanations" of why their marriage will not work and why they had good reason to behave the way they did. Since my approach focuses on the future, not on the past, the most useful information came from the Emotional Needs Questionnaire, the Love Busters Questionnaire, and the Love Bank Inventory. These told me, respectively, what they needed from each other, what they did to hurt each other, and how much romantic love they had for each other.

The assessment led to the development of a plan to overcome Art and Pam's marital conflicts. I encouraged them individually to (a) learn to meet the most important emotional needs of their spouse and (b) avoid being the cause of their spouse's unhappiness. From the results of the questionnaires, I described the emotional needs to be met and the love busters to be avoided.

Sometimes I wait a few weeks before encouraging clients to meet each other's emotional needs. If the two are in the state of emotional withdrawal, they do not want their needs met by the other, and I must help them overcome love busters before there is a willingness to be emotionally vulnerable enough to consider having the other meet their needs. But Art and Pam were in the state of emotional conflict, so it was appropriate to emphasize need fulfillment immediately.

Art and Pam were guilty of two love busters—angry outbursts and disrespectful judgments. The most important emotional need that Art had failed to meet for Pam was affection, and the most important emotional need that Pam had failed to met for Art was admiration. Since they had not been meeting each other's most important emotional needs, they both had been frustrated and had expressed their resentment toward each other with anger and disrespect.

Their love bank balances were depleted, and they both found little reason to remain married, except for the belief that it was not God's will for them to divorce. But even that belief was fading fast.

Pam and Art's first assignment was to read chapters 2 and 3 ("Angry Outbursts" and "Disrespectful Judgments") in *Love Busters* and chapters 1, 2, 3, and 12 ("Introduction," "Love Bank," "Affection," and "Admiration") in *His Needs, Her Needs*. It was quite a bit of material to cover, so I recommended one chapter a day. I have a workbook, which is not presently in print, that guides clients through these chapters, and both Art and Pam were expected to complete these workbook assignments. I gave a copy of each of my books to Art and Pam and encouraged them to use a highlighter, one color for Pam and another for Art, to underscore sentences that were important to them.

Before the couple left the assessment, I gave each of them another Love Bank Inventory to complete just before their next session. For the remainder of therapy, I would have them complete this form on the day before each treatment session but not share it with each other. The results enabled me to evaluate the effectiveness of the treatment plan. If the results of the inventory improved during treatment, I would stay with the original plan. But if the results did not improve, I would change the plan or redirect my effort.

At the end of the assessment, I went with Art and Pam to the receptionist to schedule them for their first therapeutic session. If a couple's relationship is extremely unstable, I schedule the first session a few days later. But for Pam and Art, I scheduled it a week later. Under almost no circumstances do I ever schedule the first session of therapy weeks after the assessment. A full schedule means I do not take new clients.

From that point on, each time Art and Pam came for therapy I trained both of them to avoid angry outbursts and disrespectful judgments and measured their success or failure. I also trained Art to meet Pam's need for affection and Pam to meet Art's need for admiration and measured their success or failure in meeting those needs. During therapy, I assume the role of a coach, training players to be highly skilled. The clients have practice sessions to develop their skill, and I measure not only the improvement of their skill but also the impact of that improvement. If all goes well, they begin depositing love units in the very first week of therapy.

When Art and Pam returned for their first therapy session, I saw them separately (a) to review their workbook assignments, (b) to determine if they felt they had been successful in avoiding angry outbursts and disrespectful judgments, (c) to determine if they had made an effort to meet each other's needs, and (d) to review their

Love Bank Inventories to measure whether or not their feelings had improved toward each other. Emphasis was placed on their own performance and not the failures of the other spouse.

Both Art and Pam did very well avoiding angry outbursts and disrespectful judgments. Once it was brought to their attention that these habits ruined any hope for marital reconciliation, they were able to stop them almost immediately. But they were poorly motivated and unskilled in meeting each other's important emotional needs. So I spent most of each counseling session describing the habits that each was to learn.

I showed Art that affection began the moment he awoke, and he learned to hug and kiss Pam the very first thing in the morning. He even brought her a glass of orange juice before she got out of bed. He reminded her that he cared for her while they ate breakfast together, and he hugged and kissed her before going to work. Art called Pam during the day to see how her day was going and again before he left work so she knew when to expect him. Once in a while, he brought flowers home with a note that expressed his care for her. Each day, when he came home from work, he took time to talk to her about her day. Art's conversation expressed his willingness to be there when she needed him because he cared about her feelings and wanted to make her happy. He helped with the dishes after dinner, and before they went to sleep, he hugged and kissed her.

It was not that Art had not cared about Pam. It was, however, that he had never learned the habits that express that care. Once Art learned those habits, Pam was very impressed, though at first she thought it was contrived, and to some extent, it was. But after a few weeks, when the habits became more natural and spontaneous, they both responded to each other with a passion that had been missing for years. Their sexual relationship improved overnight, so to speak, and Pam reported that she no longer had problems reaching an orgasm.

I taught Pam how to be an admiring wife. She had the skills of criticism down to a science, and the only way she knew how to avoid disrespectful judgments was to say nothing at all. I wanted her to learn to be respectful *while* Art was learning the skills of affection.

So even though her most important need was not being met, she was to be as admiring as possible.

Pam and I spent each session thinking about Art's value to her and how she could express it to him. She made lists of Art's characteristics that she appreciated: he was a committed Christian and loved the Lord; he was intelligent; he was neat and clean; he was ambitious and earned a good income; he was physically fit and good-looking; and he was dependable. Each day she reminded herself of his value to her and tried to express to him the things she appreciated about him. Even though her efforts were often forced and sometimes unconvincing, Art needed her admiration so badly that he did not mind at all. In fact, he gave her credit for simply trying, and she came to realize that there was much about him that she really did appreciate. Before long, Art and Pam were depositing love units by the trainload, and I watched their scores on the Love Bank Inventory increase almost every time I saw them.

The duration of a couple's therapy depends on how far they have fallen into the well. Some couples are out in a few weeks while others take months before romantic love has returned. Art and Pam were in love with each other within three months of the intake session. After seeing them each week for three weeks, I lengthened the time between sessions, seeing them a total of ten times in those three months. For two years, I checked on them every six months and saw that their scores on the Love Bank Inventory remained high. When they were finally discharged, I gave them the results of all their Love Bank Inventories from the beginning so that they could see how their marriage had improved.

Once Art and Pam were in love with each other, their conflicts were handled in a caring and thoughtful way. Evening conversations were enthusiastic and mutually interesting. Their secondary problems seemed to melt away. Their past problems rarely, if ever, came to mind. Art and Pam's marriage was restored because they learned to meet each other's needs and avoided being the cause of each other's unhappiness.

Task 2
Create a dialogue between the counselor and the couple (or one spouse, if you prefer) showing how you might deal with communication difficulties.

Much of my counseling is persuasive in nature. That is, I try to convince couples to give my approach to their marriage a chance. The following dialogue is an illustration of how Pam and I would talk to each other in one of the early therapy sessions when she is not convinced that she should try to be respectful and admiring. My conversational style with Art would be similar, but we would focus on his issues.

"Hi, Pam. How did you do this week?"

Pam comes with notes she took so that she can remember points she wants me to address.

"I was very upset with Art on Tuesday. You told me not to say anything 'disrespectful,' so I just kept quiet, but he didn't read the assignment like you told him to. Why should I work on our marriage when he doesn't care a bit about it?"

Pam was about to go to her next point, but I cut her off before she could begin. "Well, I'll be talking to Art in just a few minutes, but right now I want to talk to you about how you did on your assignment. Let's begin with angry outbursts. Did you lose your temper at all this past week?"

"Just once," she said. "If you were raised in an Italian home, you'd realize that it's the way we express ourselves. It would be like me telling you not to breathe. It can't be done!"

"I think you'd agree with me that when your mother and father lose their tempers, they're hurting each other. As a child, didn't you wish they wouldn't do that to each other? Didn't you wish they would show more care for each other than that?"

"Yes," she admitted. "But I eventually decided that it was one of the necessary evils of marriage, and that after losing their tempers, they'd make it up to each other. But Art doesn't like to fight, so he runs off like a coward and hides behind his precious computer. One of these days I'll see to it that it says its last 'beep,' and then where will he run?"

"I admit you know how to hurt him," I said, "but is that what you want to do the rest of your lives, hurt each other?"

"OK, OK. I won't hurt the little boy this week. But as you can see, I don't have much patience. He'd better improve fast."

"By next week at this time will you be able to tell me that you didn't lose your temper once?" I asked.

"I think so," she said. "Now can I tell you what bothered me this week?"

"Not yet," I cautioned. "Were you able to avoid disrespectful judgments?"

"Yes, except when I lost my temper," she admitted. "When I wasn't mad, I just buttoned my lip."

For Pam to successfully button her lip was an achievement of major proportions. She had been accustomed to saying whatever she felt, and what she felt lately was all negative when it came to Art.

"Do you know what will happen to me next week?" she asked.

Before I had a chance to answer, she said, "I'll probably explode. I'll have a breakdown. At the very least I'll have a headache. It's unhealthy to keep your feelings all bottled up. I need to tell Art how upset I am with him."

"All I want you to do is avoid hurting Art," I responded. "I want you to be able to express your feelings to him, but I want you to learn to do it in a way that doesn't hurt him. Doesn't that make sense?"

She agreed, and before she could complain again, I asked her, "Now, let's talk about admiration. Does Art do anything that you value? Can you think of anything you admire about him?"

"I can think of things I *don't* admire about him!" she answered. "Do you want to hear them? No, I don't think you would. You're no fun at all!"

"Last week, I asked you to make a list of things that you respected about Art. Did you make that list?" I inquired.

"No, I didn't," she answered. "All I could think of was Art in bed with Lisa, and that ruined all my respect."

Pam was trying to excuse her behavior based on events of the past. It was true that Art had an affair, but I never allow a client to "explain" his or her failures in terms of a spouse's failures.

"You mean to tell me that since Art had the affair, he's never done anything you respect?" I asked. "Think about it a minute. Tell me something that Art does that you value."

"Well, I respect him for being a Christian. But why would a Christian have an affair?"

"Christians sometimes make mistakes just like non-Christians. You're a Christian, and you make mistakes, too," I said. "Think of something else you respect about him."

I tried to move the conversation along so Pam would not dwell on her feeling that having an affair was an unforgivable mistake.

"I think he's good at fixing things around the house, and I'm glad he's not lazy like my brother, Ed. I don't know how Kathy puts up with him."

"Can you think of anything else?" I asked.

"Yes, but I'll let you talk to Art now," she said. "I don't want to use up our time talking to me 'cause he's the one that really needs the help."

"All right," I agreed, "but next time will you show me a list of ten things you appreciate about Art and tell him about each of them before you see me? OK?"

"OK," Pam said, and I took her to the waiting room where Art was ready to see me.

From this description of how a session of mine might go, it is possible to make several observations:

1. I spend very little time on the subject of communication, for I assume that the couple's conversations will improve when they learn how to meet each other's emotional needs and avoid being the cause of each other's unhappiness. Once they begin expressing care for each other in the habits they form and learn to avoid, they are able to communicate with care and compassion, and their problems are resolved with each other's feelings in mind.

2. I try to explain my approach to the couple's problem, but proof is in the outcome of therapy, not in my arguments. I do not require that clients agree with me. They simply must do what I recommend: Meet each other's needs and avoid being the cause of each other's unhappiness.

3. My clients are discouraged from complaining about the behavior of their spouse. The focus of attention during therapy is each one's own behavior and how it affects his or her spouse. The best way they can complain is through the Love Bank Inventory. If the score improves, I assume the spouse is doing a good job learning how to care for the other. But if the score remains the same, improvement in the spouse's behavior is needed.

4. I maintain control of the counseling session and focus attention on creating habits that demonstrate care and compassion. When a husband and wife are in my office together, I do not allow them to argue with each other, but rather to use the opportunity to practice the skills they are learning to demonstrate their thoughtfulness.

5. My goal is to save the marriage with romantic love restored to both individuals. I hold myself accountable for the outcome, considering failure to be due to my inability to (a) motivate the couple, (b) help control their emotional reactions, or (c) provide an effective solution. I consider marriage counseling to be no different in terms of outcome than plumbing or dentistry. When a couple with a marital problem comes to a counselor, the counselor should be able to guide them through their crisis to a solid relationship. If the counselor has another objective, such as encouraging divorce, or if he or she lacks the

skills to help them restore love for each other, they should be referred to someone more suitable.

I no longer operate mental-health clinics in Minnesota, but I conduct marriage workshops for counselors and couples, write curricula for marriage courses, and design strategies to help couples overcome specific marital problems. I hope, eventually, to complete a series of "idea" books that describe the variety of ways I have seen couples resolve each of a series of common marital conflicts.

My father's advice turned out to be right on target. My passion for understanding marriage and solving marital problems was the career I would have chosen if I had been financially independent, and what a great career it has been!

References

Festinger, L. 1957. *A theory of cognitive dissonance.* New York: Harper and Row.

Harley, W. F., Jr. 1986. *His needs, her needs: Building an affair-proof marriage.* Grand Rapids: Fleming H. Revell.

———. 1992. *Love busters: Overcoming the habits that destroy romantic love.* Grand Rapids: Fleming H. Revell.

———. 1994. *Five steps to romantic love: A workbook for readers of "Love busters" and "His needs, her needs."* Grand Rapids: Fleming H. Revell.

Kaplan, H. S. 1974. *The new sex therapy: Active treatment of sexual dysfunctions.* New York: Brunner/Mazel.

Additional Resources

For the complete Love Bank Inventory, write or call: 12568 Ethan Avenue North, White Bear Lake, Minnesota 55130 (612-429-6729). For articles, questionnaires, and general information, visit Dr. Harley's home page on the World Wide Web at http://www.marriage-builders.com.

Foundational Understandings
in Marriage Counseling

Donald M. Joy

Question 1
What are the basics of your theory of marriage counseling? In your description, include your view of the typical cause(s) of marital problems and the typical goals of counseling.

By biblical, pastoral, structural-developmental theory, I mean a highly coherent and compatible set of foundational understandings inherent in two factors: (a) The unfolding biblical revelation of God in history in which creation design stands in contrast to human sin and default, yet the sovereign God invests sovereign responsibility in image-of-God humans. (b) A pastoral vocation that seeks to connect deep human yearnings to the affirming revelation of God using empowering strategies and trusting the people to do the work of making meaning of their own lives and circumstances and responding to the divine initiatives of grace and hope. By *structural*, I refer to the internal created structures in all human beings by which we invent language, make meaning, and unravel deep issues of justice, affection, and survival in predictable, sequential ways—knowledge of which amounts to a road map of paths to recovery and fulfillment of the human vision and potential. I also want to suggest by the word *structural* that each person is engaged in "constructing" meaning in attaching new experience to older, more familiar memories and meanings, and in creating new categories to house expanding perceptions. By *developmental*, I refer to the lifelong pilgrimage on which each person has embarked. In any conversation, I look for markers along the way that will tell me what territory a parishioner/client is currently traversing so as to join the person in the journey as a companion and occasional guide.

Foundational Assumptions

My first foundational assumption is that the "image of God . . . , male and female" (Gen. 1:27 NIV) constitutes God's original witness to us—God's image became flesh. The "image of God" in sexual differentiation not only provides a universal disclosure of the nature of God's being, but also is the intrinsic magnet that draws male and female toward each other. That magnetic pull, visible in human pair-bonding behavior and emotions, operates out of energy occasioned by the Creator's "splitting of the Adam" out of isolation into sexual differentiation. Whether, then, I am dealing with young love in its magnetic early bonding in premarriage consultation and training or dealing with a troubled marriage, I ground my perspective in this image-of-God view of their relationship and construct couple experiences calculated to enhance the image-of-God gifts they bring to each other. Understandably, sexual infidelity or violation constitutes an especially crucial trauma, since sexuality carries the "image of

God" and since distortion, deformity, or default into self-serving sexual behaviors constitutes the ultimate blasphemy against the divine nature and purposes in the universe.

My second foundational assumption is that God's first commandment to humans, male and female, is to "have dominion" (Gen. 1:26). The sovereign God has created humans as sovereigns and marriage, which is modeled on the Trinity, as a co-regency of empowered, "one flesh" (Gen. 2:24) sovereigns. I hold a trinitarian view of marriage and family, in classical patristic tradition, that the father-mother-child family is modeled on the Father-Son-Spirit community. In that three-in-one intimacy, a common hope and a mutual interdependency denote their common essence. In a trinitarian marriage and family structure, individuals retain identity, but a mystery of union occurs when they are "couple" or "family," the best of all ways of "being," created in the image of God's Being.

My third assumption is that all of us are broken, that we live in a broken universe, and that our spontaneous responses to relational emergencies tend to follow a fatal pattern by which we mangle, mutilate, and kill the very thing we want to restore. This reality plank in my theoretical/theological foundation keeps me alert to hone my pastoral surgical skills. I resist allowing a negative view of humanity to dominate my work with anyone. I confess that I am an evangelist, one incurably focused on seeing good-news potential for everyone. So my reality acceptance of tragedy is tempered by my energized search for a way out, for reconstruction, for transformation, for a way "up."

A fourth assumption is that by careful listening I will be able to discover some positive hope in which to "hook" a life-enrichment line. When Susan came asking whether she was justified in seeking a divorce from her husband, I affirmed her search: "It was your integrity that brought you from out of state to ask the question. This means that you will not be easily satisfied by any decision that lacks integrity."

My fifth assumption is that the client or parishioner who comes for help has sufficient energy to make the right decisions and to take steps toward living out the decisions. When I was twenty-nine, it finally dawned on me: "There is one Savior and that is enough." I saw clearly that I had been a rescuer, loving too much and actually further disabling people who were trusting me with their life pain. In structural-developmental theory, we speak of "empowering" people and of affirming their ability to "make meaning" and to create and own decisions. Such a theory offers a very high view of the value and integrity of persons.

A sixth assumption of my work consists of affirming people in the good work they have been doing in defining their feelings and in counting the costs of the failure or the abuse. "Whatever you are feeling is OK," I find myself saying to people who are in the grasp of some pain, "and I will stick with you while you develop some 'constructive' strategy for sorting out your own issues from issues of other principals involved and in finding a way of action on those feelings so that you can get the thing you want most of all."

The preceding two foundational assumptions are back-burner agenda items that I assess from first contact. This seventh foundational assumption is similar: The general physiological well-being of the client/parishioner may be playing a significant role in the presenting problem. Since I take the creation very seriously, I am keenly aware of the great leverage of general physical wellness over emotional and spiritual complaints and disabilities. One of my students popped in quickly to say, "Doc, I think I've got a problem. My wife is very depressed. Could you talk to her today?" Of course I could. After taking notes for about twenty minutes as she described her feelings of hopelessness and self-doubt, I asked, "Are you ovulating regularly?" Her unusual response quickly prompted me to refer her to an ob-gyn physician and to make the initial call to his office. Her irregular ovulation since pubescence was a clue about potential links with depression. The side effects of some contraceptive pills include mood alteration, reduced interest in sexual contact, and general depression. Any symptoms of bipolar disorders and of many forms of depression deserve an immediate referral to a medical doctor.

Finally, as an eighth comprehensive foundation, I quickly try to discover what piece of the systemic puzzle this client/parishioner may be presenting. To whom else do I need to speak to check the role, status, value pieces of the total picture? Until I have gathered perspectives and data from the spouse and sometimes from other people living in the same domicile, I cannot be sure whether I have been looking at the problem or at a symptom of a deeper problem, perhaps one outside the identified client/parishioner.

Typcial Causes of Marital Problems

In rank order, these are the most common presenting problems in marital distress: (a) current sexual intimacy dysfunction or frustration, including compulsive or sexual addiction disorders; (b) premarital sexual activity either with each other or with other partners (couples who lived together prior to marriage pose a unique set of marital problems and recovery challenges); (c) current sexual infidelity, an affair; and a distant fourth (d) financial distress, most often grounded in abused credit and extravagant consumption appetites accompanied by exorbitant interest and tax delinquencies.

Three domains of marital synchrony seem urgent in premarital or postmarital counseling. First, I am eager to assess how each partner has been received by the other's family. Here, a check of perceptions each has regarding the other's parents and extended family, of their acceptance of the new potential for actual family acquisition by marriage, and of their sense of comfort or ambivalence about patterns of family life and ways of relating are very useful for reflection. Next, I check perceptions and practices about the use of money. This is partly an extension of each family's understanding of money, but it is a present reality, too. The partners have had an opportunity to evaluate each other's ways of acquiring and spending money. Synchronizing their expectations on the money issue will predict smoother sailing throughout the marriage. Finally, in premarriage consulting, I design one session to listen to the couple's history of magnetic attraction. This serves as a way to introduce the mystery of human bonding and the magic of the slow development of the pair-bond, which cements a couple for lifelong exclusive intimacy.

Never do I ask a premarital couple for a report on their sexual experiences. From counseling videos or the pair-bonding background reading, the couple will be aware of the confidential disclosures couples make who do solid pair-bonding work. I will remind the couple of these disclosures, pointing out that their worst worries deserve to be entrusted now, during the engagement, while a solid base of trust is forming. I take the position that every couple's journey of intimacy belongs to the two of them only and that any disclosure to anyone about the journey constitutes a leakage of their confidential intimacy. I have observed that pastoral or counselor invasion of this privacy tends to produce sexual-abuse effects and to weaken the pair-bond of the couple.

When sexual experience in the relationship is reported to me out of a need to resolve guilt or regain integrity in the relationship, I work toward enveloping the premature, or otherwise inappropriate, sexual misadventure, helping the couple to a solid and healthy confession, while at the same time salvaging the "gold," sanctifying it, and bringing it forward into the marital bond. When secrets have been spilled as a means of urgent relief or of naming a marital or premarital problem, I initiate a liturgy of "returning the secrets" and urge the couple to keep them forever as a treasure within their confidential and holy interior-sanctuary—such confidential material is epoxy glue within their mysterious pair-bond.

When marital distress is a presenting issue, I suggest that the couple revisit the formation of their marital and sexual bond. Positive revisiting tends to enhance strengths, and it may also identify incomplete pair-bonding work agendas. I pay close attention to the couple's eye contact and other visible markers of the status and strength of the bond as I watch them do this reconstructive revisitation of their longitudinal relationship. In marital counseling, the revisitation is often a threshold through which to bring the couple into recovery of the journey into intimacy, which may have been derailed because of lack of attention to the treasure of the bond they began to build. Marital distress is always visible by noting, in a reverse use of the pair-bonding model, where the damaged bond is "stuck." The couple then works in earlier bonding-stage memory to restart the bond and generate enough energy to renegotiate the steps that had been abandoned out of desperate self-protection.

With a couple approaching marriage, I schedule a final session only a few days before the wedding. If specific questions about sexual intimacy and adjustment do not arise, I describe the baffling mystery of sex differences, the mirror design of the female "process system" in relation to the male "hydraulic system," the differences between the male and female pleasure systems, and the typical missed communications these differences tend to produce. While the female biological clock of ovulation and menstruation is widely known, it is rarely considered that the woman's entire reproductive system may do its work without sexual arousal or pleasure. In contrast the male hydraulic system guarantees that orgasmic pleasure occurs in the delivery of male fertility: sperm. Every male, ejaculating frequently since the onset of pubescence, comes to sexual intimacy with previous pleasure experience.

In that final premarital session, I outline the probable path of the groom's sexual pleasure awakening, project to the development of full sexual appetite, and indicate that young men may evacuate their system frequently in very different ways. The more serious males tend to abstain from intercourse and often feel the baffling shame associated with self-stimulation. Family and church silence on male sexuality may leave males at the mercy of the electronic media, which encourages them to be penetrating as soon as their curiosity awakens. Whatever the pattern, I urge the couple to be prepared on the honeymoon to present to each other a full disclosure of sexual exploration and experience. I provide them with a one-page Honeymoon Agenda, which offers strategies to discover ways of matching their intimacy with the maximum potential frequency of sexual intercourse.

I have instituted this early marriage shakedown of honesty in pleasure appetites after dealing with explosive wives who regarded their husbands' masturbatory patterns as the basis for ending the marriages. Yet the wives often had been resisting frequent sexual intimacy, regarded the husbands as "dirty" or "oversexed," and sometimes viewed the husbands as a threat to young sons the women were rearing. "So, did your father ever tell you at thirteen to stop ovulating and menstruating, to just wait until you were married to do that silly stuff?" I have inquired of some of them. Others have heard me ask: "And if you knew your thirteen-year-old son's 'tiger in the tank' was producing 300 million sperm every few days, what would you say to him? If his full adult sexual appetite is developed by thirty-six months after first ejaculation, what do you want him to do with it? What did your husband do with his production and energy between thirteen and his wedding day? What do you want him to do with it now that he is married? Do you stop ovulating except when you want a baby?"

When a couple is able to meet my ideal of a marriage-preparation schedule, I urge a combination of a marriage-preparation retreat or seminar along with three premarriage pastoral sessions and two sessions soon after the wedding. That is, I suggest two sessions at intervals of one month, with a fourth on sexual intimacy and the honeymoon agenda within days or hours of the wedding. But I also request a session immediately following the honeymoon, or within two weeks if the couple remains local. And I ask to see them in three months. At those sessions I review the areas of grounding: family of origin and relationships there; view and use of money; bonding and consummation of intimacy in a positive pattern.

Question 2
For what kind of people is your approach most appropriate?

Working as I do from a biblical, pastoral, structural-developmental base, I find that people of virtually all circumstances and cultures and developmental ages are comfortable doing their constructive work with me. I always try to work "systemically" with a client, taking a reading on the presenting problem in the presence of all members of the household, sometimes including family members beyond the present house. Only after such a reading am I comfortable working in individual construction sessions as both spouses, and sometimes family members, envision and design strategies to enhance the potential for achieving health for everyone.

The biblical, pastoral, structural-developmental approach is useful in teaching, preaching, and therapeutic consulting in a variety of settings, for example, in consulting sessions, workshops, and seminars. Since it empowers people to do their own work, the teacher's-pastor's-counselor's task is reduced from having to do the healing to coaching people who are healed as they go. Indeed, such an approach prevents the pastor or counselor from assuming a neurotic role as a client's savior, in which inappropriate dependence is easily developed, and instead fosters the release of the client to return to his or her own home and show what great things God is doing in the client's life.

Question 3
What are your foci for counseling?

Let me describe three foci grounded on the foundational assumptions. First, I am eager to create space and comfort that invite candor and a sense of optimism. Second, especially during the inventory and audit as I take information and organize the data with a view to recommending referral to medical treatment, therapy, or a support network, I document that what is reported is well within the range of issues that people deal with effectively. This anti-isolation strategy provides the client with immediate courage to continue with the work of healing or recovery. Third, since each person's journey and story are unique, I often ask that a writing-and-documentary phase begin at once. Honest writing, for the client's eyes only, is my most-used recommendation for releasing subjective emotions and intrusive thoughts. Because the resulting "objective" form of the feelings effectively transforms the emotions into an external document, feelings that once controlled the person are now under his or her physical control. But a second benefit has a basis in neurological energy release; memories held in electrical suspension in the brain now effectively unload onto a permanent hard-copy document. The common responses are (a) an awareness of additional old and forgotten memories that can be expelled onto paper as the dominating major traumas are first released—much like the magician's silk handkerchiefs that seem attached to an unending string of others—and (b) a sense of relief that one need not waste energy remembering important past painful memories, since they are written down and can be consulted whenever any piece of information needs to be retrieved for any reason.

During the writing phase, I ask for occasional oral reports and summaries, but insist that the written document is for the client's eyes only. A document written for any other person's eyes inevitably is distorted and less than candid and honest. And getting to the "root" requires frankness and language essential to carrying the emotional freight that needs to be dumped into objective form. I advise that the resulting document—ranging from a few to more than six hundred pages in my recent practice—be sealed, signed, and labeled so as never to be exposed to other eyes.

Question 4
How is your marriage counseling conducted?

I am eager to take an audit of any perceived marital problem. I explain that this one session will provide an opportunity for me to recommend what sort of strategies may be most helpful: "If you have an apparent deep therapeutic need, I can recommend a specialist in your geographic area with whom you might do intensive therapy." Before I begin to listen, I ask for a Myers-Briggs (M-B) personality profile reading. With that in hand, I can "come alongside" and listen within a personality structural framework as I take copious coded notes. The note taking keeps me from dominating with my own talking and allows me to begin to construct questions, the responses to which will expand my understanding of the issue under scrutiny.

After the audit, I am generally able to suggest to the client a path to comfort and confidence. In many cases, I simply empower the individual or couple to carry forward with as-needed consultations for further brainstorming and coaching or to explore three options from among which, or from a newly emerging option, the individual or couple will develop an action plan that is workable. When I see an identifiable and persisting symptom, I recommend medical or emotional therapy and describe more than one physician or therapist and the style and strategy the client might expect to find with each. Occasionally, I suggest that we need another data-collection and strategy-exploration session, although I much prefer to do the inventory audit and exploration of next options in one extended session, if possible. In systemic unraveling, I occasionally recommend a separate session with each spouse as the second and third session, wrapping up with a fourth in which both articulate their yearnings and their proposed strategies for embracing new and healthy territory in the relationship. After this, I remain ready for future coaching consultations. It is common in such cases that I will ask for a phone-in report after a week of experimenting with a given new strategy. And I occasionally take the pastoral initiative and make the call myself to inquire how the new strategies are working.

Question 5
How do you deal with a few of the common marital problems?

The Other Woman

Lila forgave Dan for his live-in history before he was a Christian, then resurrected the ghost of the competing woman three years into the marriage. Dan had initiated the consultation. Lila was dissolved in grief that Dan had been with the other woman for longer than they had now been married. She worried that the other woman was a better sex partner than she. Two other counselors had told Lila that it was "her problem," that she needed to "forget it." I suggested that if the issue was important to her, it would not simply go away on such a command. "Whatever you feel is OK," I told her, "but it is not OK for you to resurrect that woman for Dan week after week. He gave her up, and in his pair-bonding schedule he told you the whole truth. You likely 'forgave' too quickly, but you acted in honest good faith with Dan." I suggested the writing strategy, for her eyes only, with the option of sealing, signing the seal, and mailing it to me for my files so that she would know she had delivered her pain to paper.

Traditional Roles from Genesis 3

Karl is at his wits' end. Betty held him responsible for supporting the family of three children, plus a street kid who needed a Christian home. Working two jobs, he still came up short, and there was no money for even small pleasures. I arranged for Robbie, my wife, to meet with Betty, Karl, and me. A woman's perspective was, I was sure, crucial. In the course of an hour of taking an audit on values and roles, I understood clearly that Betty was a Genesis 3 woman who had married and placed her complete hope—her "desire" (Gen. 3:16)—in her man. This "Baal marriage," which God abhors in Hosea 2:16, is a central tendency of good women.

Karl had dutifully tried to walk on water and to support the family, and Betty's heroic ways of stretching a meager income were commendable. But the crisis came when Karl turned bitter and angry, vicious and short-tempered in his scarce time with Betty and the children. He had accepted the Genesis 3 macho description of universal man: "he will rule over" the woman (v. 16). In our early years of marriage, my wife and I found ourselves revisiting our own misunderstanding of the doctrine of creation, generating similar role impossibilities, so empathy for Betty and Karl came easily. We had parallel starvation stories, but ours had not extended for eight years, as had theirs. So we congratulated them for surviving and offered them the creation roles of "having dominion" according to image-of-God gifts, instead of the sin-and-curse roles of Genesis 3.

Abuse Triggers Mental "Blame"

Ron was a victim of mentor rape at fourteen. He worried because he had responded sexually to the surprise seduction in the remote campsite with the college professor. He was sure that he, too, was gay. So within a year he initiated date intercourse and pursued intercourse with a dozen or more women by the age of twenty-four. Profoundly converted, he went to a Christian college, fell in love with a campus spiritual leader, and became sexual with her. The presenting problem was a dysfunctional, frozen-up marriage, reported by a lonely woman seeing her marriage dissolve before her eyes.

In the audit-inventory of the couple's pair history, the premarital blame landed squarely and alone on Ron. He accepted it and expressed regret that he had lost his magnetic feelings for his wife. When I asked for a separate audit on Ron's history, the rape appeared with great embarrassment. But it was a key. Ron did the work, and I did the coaching as he constructed a positive set of discoveries about the character of God from his image-of-God sexual gift.

Promiscuity—Symptom of Early Abuse

Joan was fondled from early childhood on by a family friend and lost her father through divorce at age six. At sixteen, she had given up a baby for adoption. When Joan was eighteen and pregnant again, her mother ordered the surgeon to do a radical hysterectomy instead of an abortion. In her early twenties, Joan contracted genital herpes, but nothing stopped her from her episodes of falling in love and into bed and of then picking up the pieces of yet another abandonment. When my wife, Robbie, and I came into her focus as caregivers, Joan was promiscuous and full of shame and had accompanying eating and dietary disorders. Robbie and I walked with Joan across a seven-year recovery in which the bottom line was always shared grief and unconditional affirmation.

Gender Confusion

Gene, at eighteen, felt like a woman trapped in a male body. In a full audit of Gene's family system I noted his place in the family, each member's way of relating to him, and the level of anxiety in the family as a whole. I asked for a separate audit session with Gene before meeting with the out-of-state family for a review of options they could consider. In the private session, I took a history of Gene's friendships reaching into full memory, a report on his pubescence and sexual development, a report on his feelings in favor of being a man compared with those in favor of being a woman. I was glad to assure Gene that he was in a good position to make the necessary decisions about what he wanted to live out for the next seventy-five years.

Infertility—Marital Dilemma

Janice, at twenty-eight, is engaged to marry. When she failed to start ovulating and menstruating by fourteen, a medical workup, including magnetic resonance imaging (MRI), disclosed that she had no womb, but had atrophied testes, with an accompanying chromosome disorder. Janice is well into the female-feminine track, with a wedding on the calendar. She is on hormonal medication, which has been prescribed since the medical findings at age fourteen. In the audit with Janice and her parents, I included a review of the pair-bonding sequence visible as the present romance developed. I asked her to describe the way she had handled her reproductive status with her fiancé. Though the couple are from another section of the country, I indicated my willingness to accept their request to have at least one session with them before and one after the marriage.

Task 1
Respond to the case study by telling precisely how you might typically treat it, in how many sessions, in what order, and with what responses by the clients throughout counseling. One restriction: Assume that between the third and fourth counseling sessions with you— regardless of what had gone on during the previous session—the couple had a major argument and come to the fourth session in some crisis.

Pam initiates the consultation. I agree to meet with her to do an intake, or audit, of the presenting problem, after which I will offer options of ways to proceed, based on her report.

Session 1

Pam reports on the marital distress. I make notes of a basic time line of Pam and Art's friendship, courtship, engagement, marriage, and postmarital disappointments; Art's one-night stand; Art's fertility deficits; and the worsening verbal battles, emotional distancing, and unequal sexual intimacy responses. I listen and make additional notes on Pam's affective state, her nonverbal messages, and her choice of language to describe both her own and Art's roles in the marriage and his part in the domestic crisis.

After I plot the time line of Art and Pam's relationship, using symbols for later revisiting of the history when both are in the office together, I open the following issues by asking questions. I ask Pam how important having children is to her, given the importance placed on bearing children by her family's Roman Catholic tradition. Another facet of this issue is Pam's perception of how Art has handled the diagnosis of his marginal fertility (evidently a sperm count of 50,000 or less). I ask specifically for verbal swatches of their worst-case exchanges of yelling and cursing and for identification of typical words coming from each player in that deadly shame game—and for the effect of Art's words on Pam.

Finally, I offer three scenarios from which Pam may choose one as a way of moving ahead:

1. Shall we plan to meet one additional session to be sure that her audit is complete?
2. I express a need to hear a similar audit of the presenting problem from Art's perspective. Will she try to arrange that, or shall I phone Art to request the meeting?
3. Is there some other next step Pam wants to suggest?

Session 2

Now it is crucial for me to complete the audit from Art's perspective. I have never found a husband to refuse this session—even if he has resolved to abandon the marriage. For reasons that relate to cultural and biological definitions of masculinity and maleness, most husbands or other male principals are inclined to believe that it is up to them to fix the relationship. When I ask to see Art, he seems pleased to be included in this data-gathering phase of the consultation.

My process with Art is similar to that with Pam in the first session. I construct the time line, and keep myself busy with note taking, affirmations, and clarifications. If the affair and the male infertility readings do not appear and are transparent in the time-line process, I will probe, as with Pam, into his family-of-origin expectations about producing children and his response to the discovery of the infertility problem. I am eager to hear from Art, as I was with Pam, the specific killer terms used in their verbal battles, again noting which curses, obscenities, or other harsh terms are typically used by whom and with what effect on him.

I suggest that we next meet together—Pam, Art, and I—within the week and ask Art to phone to verify or negotiate an acceptable time. I outline a proposed agenda for the next session, noting that we will revisit their friendship from the beginning, and that I will offer feedback on Myers-Briggs polarities, which may throw helpful light on some of their developing sorrow and frustration in the marriage. I provide Art with response sheets and test booklets for Myers-Briggs and indicate that the secretary can score them in less than five minutes if he and Pam will bring them back completed. I advise him that they should take the tests quickly, without brooding over the items, and should relax since the results are most helpful when the individuals give casual and honest responses to the items. I tell Art, "You'll look good and most like your real selves if you each relax and 'undress' on paper with the inventory. No response has a right or wrong inference, as you will see."

Session 3

I welcome Art and Pam and turn their response sheets over to the secretary for scoring while we begin our review of the early history of their attraction to each other. Following my explanation of the pair-bonding steps, I invite them to describe in detail and in sequence their memories and remembered feelings of (a) their first sightings of each other and any traces of magnetic pull to "look again," (b) their first words to each other, (c) their first touch, (d) their first confidential secrets and the effect of that trust, and (e) their first, or other early, sexual contact. This revisitation to high points of positive memory allows Art and Pam to do their own affirmation of their exclusive marital bond—the treasure they are now finding reduced to an obligation, a duty, even a moral and religious prison. The positive memory-walk tends to provide them and me with indicators of the depth and quality of the bond that undergirds them in the present distress. The anecdotal material also throws light on the possibility that the magic in the relationship was profoundly enhanced by their differences, a discovery they may be ready to make as they review their Myers-Briggs personality profile preferences.

When Art's and Pam's memory walk is completed, I summarize and identify the indestructible bonding contributions each has made to the marriage. I go on the side of the angels to predict that with Art's and Pam's good work done early in the relationship, there are new high grounds to be taken as they move toward creating a new marriage to replace the old one, which has gotten bogged down with pain and conflict and criticism of each other.

I then sketch Pam's and Art's M-B raw scores and letters on my chalkboard:

Pam			Art		
22	E	5	6	I	20
19	S	8	10	N	12
9	F	12	12	T	11
20	J	7	12	J	9

I characterize the M-B profile as descriptive like a photograph—presenting useful comparisons to what each knows is true of himself or herself—and I distinguish the profile from prescriptive measures, which might have suggested some change or improvement. I describe the M-B polarities as indicating where each is likely to find most energy and spontaneity in doing the therapeutic work. In short, each letter suggests a personal preference that is a gift easily presented to each other and to other people. The raw numbers simply suggest that those items that were completed have a sort of "weight" for the preference—some almost "tied" between the polarities, others were profoundly preferred.

As a wrap-up for this session, I summarize the polar opposites that attracted Art and Pam in the beginning. I make an evaluation (always affirming) of their resources to build on these polar-opposite gifts, and I offer to coach them in their journey toward enhancing that solid relationship into a super marriage. Finally, we agree on an appointment time for about a week away.

Session 4

When Pam and Art arrive for this session, it is clear that a cloud has come over both of them. As I inquire about their experiment in seeing each other as "beloved opposites," Art reports that he has hurt Pam and that the wound may have been fatal.

For about two days, the experiment proved to be a good experience. In fact, it was so good that Art revisited memories of shared secrets from the time when he and Pam were negotiating when to announce their engagement and marriage. During the revisiting, Art expressed regret that they had moved into such intense planning that he neglected to carve out the time or place to confess that he had been sexual in three relationships during college, one of them extending into his early dating with Pam. Pam became enraged, declared that Art had been a liar and that she now wanted out of the marriage because she had "grounds." Most of this session is absorbed with coaching Art to revisit and reconstruct the prime-opportunity time when he wanted to make a bond of truth with Pam about his previous sexual activity, then coaching Pam to respond to him as she might have responded if she had heard it before the engagement went public. With the strength of that remembered early trust, the two of them leave, agreeing to return in a week to look for ways to put their strength to work both celebrating their newly discovered level of vulnerability and honesty, as well as their unique differences, and exploring ways to package their gifts so as not to be abrasive to each other.

Task 2
Create a dialogue between the counselor and the couple (or one spouse, if you prefer) showing how you might deal with communication difficulties.

After the time line of Art's and Pam's relationship is nearly completed, I want to explore the precise language and the emotional charge that seem to be unleashed when Art and Pam have their occasional firefights. Both Pam and Art have referred to them. I interrogated Pam along these lines of specificity near the end of my audit session with her. Now I open the issue with Art:

Joy: Both you and Pam have referred to some pretty ugly fights you have once in a while.

Art: Yeah. They are not pretty.

Joy: Can you close your eyes and revisit the last one, or the worst one? I want to hear the soundtrack of who says what. And I want you to see whether you can reconstruct your feelings as you describe what was going on.

Art: I'll try. I'm not proud that we do this, you know.

Joy: We all have a potential dark side, but sometimes if we can discover the fuel that is ignited, we can get that energy into more productive work in another way.

Art: I guess the last time was, actually, the worst. The fights seem to get worse each time. Pam really blew up when she saw me drive up in a new car. I had known for several months that the prime time for trading—you know, with replacing tires and winterizing it coming up—would be about now. I always take care of the transportation and outdoor decisions. So I made the best deal in town, and I traded. Pam went into histrionics! She called me everything but a child of God.

Joy: What did she call you? What were the words?

Art: I don't like to repeat them. You know we don't talk like that

81

around other people—only when we're yelling at each other.

Joy: Did she grow up hearing violent verbal assaults between her parents at home? Kids don't miss much, you know.

Art: Yeah. She uses the God language when she's really mad, and they do, too. After I got into the family, I overheard some of the violence between her parents—just like her words. You know they are really very religious words, but the anger just turns them blue. [*Here Art reluctantly repeated Pam's alleged words directed at him, the ones damning him to hell and the S words used to describe how dirty and rotten Art was to do a thing like that.*]

Joy: Good work. I know those are unpleasant words, but we can speculate about that "pedigree" she has plastered on you and where it may be coming from. Now what about you? What killer words do you use on Pam?

Art: I hate myself for this. And you'll never respect me when I tell you the way I talk to Pam sometimes. When I go ballistic, I use the F word and tell her where to take her f— ideas, her f— mouth.

Joy: That is pretty tough talk. Can you describe what you are feeling when this volatile energy cuts loose?

Art: You know, I feel trapped, powerless, and I know I'm not the man I set out to be. I feel really rotten, so I yell to cover up how rotten I feel.

Joy: You mentioned how disappointed you were that the fertility problem turned out to be yours, not Pam's.

Art: I try not to think about that. It's pretty depressing to think I'll never see my own flesh and blood.

Joy: When you were thirteen or so, how much did you think about being a sexual person? Was that important to you?

Art: It was very important—and still is. But I was supposed to be a good kid, you know. I figured it was wrong, but I released myself a lot during those years and always felt there was something wrong with me. I thought so much about it.

Joy: When did the F word show up in your vocabulary?

Art: The first year I went out for basketball—eighth grade. I guess we were all pretty hot with sexual development—as I remember what I was seeing and hearing in the locker room. There were magazines in lockers, and the word was often used when we were thinking about sex, but we used it when we were mad or when we had a big game coming up. It was hard to know what the word really meant. I'm not sure I know even now. Because the only time I use it is when I'm really p—— off! There's another one! Why do sexual words get used to ventilate my anger?

Joy: I think you're getting to the root of the reason. Young men who don't get intimacy and anger sorted out by about age fifteen are likely to confuse them for the rest of their lives. In the worst case scenario, they think "sex is violence, and violence is sex." But by age forty men who have not surrendered the sexual words for violence often can't perform in sexual intimacy—because the testosterone levels eliminate the quick arousal and performance that worked well under adrenaline when they were younger.

Art: Can I get it sorted out at thirty-eight?

Joy: The timing is on your side. And I think you can, now that you've named the confusion. But you will want to go back and bless that thirteen- or fifteen-year-old kid and tell him he was just right, fresh from the Creator's hand, fully charged sexually. If you can bless that aroused and awakened kid and put intimacy words on what he was feeling, I'm sure you can sanctify everything between here and there. That should take away a lot of shame and frustration.

Art: You mean the shame I feel for talking to Pam like that?

Joy: That, too, of course, but I was talking about the shame that drives you when you feel rotten, worthless, and less than a man. That deep feeling of inadequacy is what drives your compensatory outbursts—trying to prove by a sort of macho take-charge swagger and voice that you are OK.

Art: I can't believe this. How could you have known how

insecure and inadequate I feel when Pam attacks me?

Joy: Your words are autobiographical. They are not about Pam. They are your weapons to bring her down to the rotten level where you are groveling. You know that you were enveloped in shame when your sexuality blossomed, that you were driven by it, but always baffled at how strong your desires were. So you got stuck in a negative sexual cloud, and your anger words revolve around things having to do with your penis.

Art: Are Pam's killer words autobiographical? How could all of those God-hell-damnation words be autobiographical?

Joy: Both you and Pam may have borrowed your killer words from other people—you from the young men in the locker room and she from her parents or other adults who used them. But Pam likely finds those words suiting her purposes because of the pathos of most women. And when a woman is gifted with personality preferences for managing things well, anger and resentment often flourish if they feel they have abandoned their internal sovereignty. Yet many women want someone to take care of them, only to find that they resent the guy who takes that bait.

Art: I thought that is what a woman wanted. In fact, I'm sure Pam always said that—even before we were married, "I want a man who will take care of me and make my decisions. I want a man with a plan!" That's what she said.

Joy: No doubt. But those lines are straight out of Genesis 3: Her "desire shall be for her husband [meaning actually, she will worship him and depend on him], and he shall rule over" her.

Art: Exactly. That's what we thought we were going to do for each other. She would trust me completely, and I would take care of her and protect her. And I would make the decisions.

Joy: You got it right, except that is the model of the cursed marriage, not God's design. God's design in Genesis 1 was, "Let them have dominion," and in Genesis 2: "[The two] shall become one." The word *one* here is the same Hebrew word used in Exodus 20, "Hear O Israel, the Lord our God is One!"

Art: But how does this fit with Pam's speaking autobiographically when all the God language mows me down?

Joy: Women don't have a corner on the negative God language, but people who use it are exercising power. They are invoking the lowest form of prayer—a demand that God do for them what they are powerless to do for themselves.

Art: How could I help Pam feel more power?

Joy: Well, I think we're going to be working on those strategies across the next few weeks, now that both of you are getting to the root of the struggle in your marriage. For starters, you might ask how you could trade in your Genesis 3 marriage for one from Genesis 1 and 2.

References

Friesen, L. W. 1989. Sexuality: A biblical model in historical perspective. Ph.D. diss., Fuller Theological Seminary.

Joy, D. M. 1990. *Becoming a man*. Ventura, Calif.: Regal Books.

———. 1994a. *Bonding: Relationships in the image of God*. Anderson: Bristol House.

———. 1994b. *Risk-proofing your family*. Pasadena, Calif.: U.S. Center for World Mission. First published as *Parents, kids, and sexual integrity*. Dallas: Word Books, 1988.

———. 1995. *Re-bonding: Preventing and restoring damaged relationships*. Anderson: Bristol House.

———. 1996. *Celebrating the new woman*. In press. Wilmore, Ken.: Center for the Family.

———, ed. 1983. *Moral development foundations: Theological alternatives to Piaget and Kohlberg*. Nashville: Abingdon.

Joy, D. M., and D. Hager. 1993. *Women at risk*. Anderson: Bristol House.

Joy. D. M., and R. B. Joy. 1994. *Lovers: What ever happened to Eden?* Dallas: Word Books.

Kegan, R. 1982. *The evolving self: Problem and process in human development*. Cambridge: Harvard University Press.

Couple Communication

Gary J. Oliver and Sherod Miller

Question 1
What are the basics of your theory of marriage counseling? In your description, include your view of the typical cause(s) of marital problems and the typical goals of counseling.

When Adam and Eve sinned in the Garden of Eden, humankind was affected in many ways, not the least of which was our ability to communicate. Sin not only erected a barrier between God and humans, but also produced relational barriers between men and women. In Genesis 3, we read that not only did Adam and Eve hide from God and each other, they also hurled or placed responsibility for their problems on the serpent, each other, and God. We have been hiding and hurling ever since.

Our experience has shown us that most failures in marriage are not caused by blowouts, but by slow leaks. One of the main contributors to slow leaks in a relationship is difficulty in communicating, or even the inability to communicate. As goes a couple's ability to communicate, so goes everything else in their relationship. The Couple Communication skills-training program (eight hours in a couples' group or six hours conjointly in private sessions) prevents slow leaks and helps repair blowouts.

Couple Communication was originally developed and researched by Sherod Miller, Elam Nunnally, and Daniel Wackman at the University of Minnesota Family Study Center. The thrust of the program focused on prevention rather than treatment—teaching couples how to discuss and resolve their own issues. Four mentors had a substantial impact on the development of the program: Reuben Hill, Virginia Satir, Sidney Jourard, and William F. Hill. Reuben Hill had a passion for family development. Satir (with whom Miller worked over a period of twenty years) operationalized esteem, process, and congruency. Jourard vanguarded the concept of self-disclosure and its role in health. William F. Hill conducted the original and seminal research on styles of communication. These teachers helped formulate many of the core insights (frameworks) and skills helpful in navigating the inevitable rapids that occur in any relationship.

Caring and communication skills are prerequisites to effective problem solving, conflict resolution, and verbally sharing affection. Every message has two component parts: attitude and behavior. Attitudes—caring or uncaring—derive from the combined beliefs, feelings, and intentions one holds. Behaviors—verbal and nonverbal actions—reflect and stem from underlying attitudes. So, messages—skilled or unskilled—exchanged between partners reflect a couple's underlying attitude toward self and partner.

Whenever a couple comes for marriage counseling, two levels of issues always exist. At the surface, there are a variety of content issues, things that bother or upset the partners, past behaviors that have been ineffective or painful, and current ways of dealing with problems that range from uncomfortable to unacceptable. Effective marriage counseling must in some ways acknowledge and address these presenting issues. However, underneath the surface of most couples' problems, there are usually several root causes of problems. One of the most frequent root causes is not a content issue but rather a process issue. It is not so much *what* couples argue about as it is *how* they argue. We have worked with numerous couples who have spent years in a dysfunctional dance of missed communications, thinking that the problem was sex or finances or in-laws when in fact one of their root problems was their inability to communicate and resolve issues effectively. Larry Hoff and William R. Miller (1981) have written that "Marriage is not a static system with inflexible roles, but rather a dynamic, changing relationship, calling for continued commitment to openness, creative use of differences and conflict, negotiation and re-negotiation of roles and norms, and continued individual and couple awareness and growth" (10).

A basic assumption underlying the Couple Communication program is that every relationship is unique. The way two people communicate and interact over time possesses its own special dynamic, making that couple different from any other relationship. Yet, another equally important assumption is that every relationship is similar to all other relationships in that all are living social systems. The processes and skills taught in the Couple Communication program spring from the theoretical insights and application of systems-theory properties and principles. A *system* is any whole with interacting parts. Systems properties and principles provide a framework for examining and understanding relationship development and dysfunction.

The following relationship principles are foundational to Couple Communication (Miller et al. 1992):

1. Partners have choices. They can argue over who caused what, or they can take responsibility and be accountable for their own behaviors.

2. It only takes one partner to change a system. When one person changes his or her behavior, the system changes (for better or for worse).
3. If each partner is focused on changing the other partner, nothing changes; the system stays stuck.
4. Small changes can make large differences.
5. If one partner recognizes that what he or she is doing is not working, he or she can stop and shift. By stopping his or her own ineffective behavior and shifting to a different, more productive behavior, he or she changes the system.
6. Process leads to outcome. The quality of how two people interact yields levels of meaningfulness, productivity, and satisfaction.
7. The nature of a relationship is up to both partners. While each partner contributes, neither is solely responsible for the entire relationship.
8. Every relationship is governed by informal and usually unspoken rules of relationship. These attitudinal and behavioral constraints/enablers develop and can be changed over time. They govern how two people relate.

With these eight principles serving as a foundation, Couple Communication has four major objectives:

1. To increase awareness of self, partner, and the relationship (properties of individuation, interconnectedness, boundaries, and synergy)
2. To teach skills for talking and listening together more effectively (information processing)
3. To improve ability to resolve conflicts (self-maintaining, directing, monitoring, and repairing)
4. To increase satisfaction with outcomes of issues and satisfaction with the relationship (purpose and efficiency)

Couple Communication takes into account the major aspects of personality. God has made us in God's own image (Gen. 1:26) with a mind, emotions, desires, and a will. All parts are important. But while many people are comfortable discussing intellectual issues, few people are comfortable or successful discussing issues that involve strong emotions. From Genesis to Revelation, we read about God's emotions: he is jealous, angry, loving, and kind, and God grieves over humans' rebellion. And we are created in his image. That means, like God, we feel and we care. In the four Gospels, we read that Christ experienced and expressed anger, distress, sorrow, disappointment, frustration, fear, amazement, love, compassion, joy, and delight. Couple Communication provides couples with a framework that helps them be aware of and understand all their God-given dimensions of personality. This tool, the Awareness Wheel, is well-grounded in psychological theory. It combines the sensate, cognitive, affective, conative, and behavioral dimensions into an integrated and practical whole. The Awareness Wheel is also a practical tool with which couples can articulate their awareness to one another.

Question 2
For what kind of people is your approach most appropriate?

Since its inception in 1968, more than five hundred thousand couples have participated in Couple Communication throughout the United States, as well as in Canada, Europe, Australia, Taiwan, and Japan. The program has been translated into five languages.

According to Karen Wampler of the Department of Human Development and Family Studies at Texas Tech University, "Couple Communication is one of the most heavily researched enrichment programs" (1990, 21). She further observed that "studies including distressed couples have documented the effectiveness of CC [Couple Communication] with these couples as well" (29). Wampler's summary and metanalysis of thirty-three independent research studies at major universities throughout the country indicates that Couple Communication is effective for a wide range of couples, including those in different social and economic groups and those of varying ages, distressed couples as well as well-functioning couples. The findings show (a) very positive impact on communication following the program, (b) increases in relationship satisfaction, and (c) enjoyment of the experience (inferred because few couples drop out).

Half of the programs have been conducted in churches; however, the conceptual frameworks, skills, and processes are effective with both Christian and non-Christian couples. Instructors come from a number of backgrounds. Most are ministers and other human-service professionals—therapists, counselors, and teachers. We have seen the program effectively applied by a wide range of instructors with a diversity of theological and theoretical orientations.

Couple Communication can best be described as psychoeducational—personal, practical, proactive, positive, and growth oriented. It can serve either an enrichment or therapy function. It fits into premarital counseling, marital therapy, marriage enrichment, or other relationship programming. The program is particularly beneficial as part of a brief-therapy treatment plan.

For example, Gary Oliver recently worked with a Christian man who wanted to confess to a lie that he had told his wife for twenty-five years regarding something he had done before they were married. Why had he waited so long? "I told her the lie when we were dating to impress her," the man explained. "Once it was out, I couldn't tell the truth for fear that she would label me a 'liar' and never trust me again. I've been a conflict-avoider all of my life, and this was just too much for me to tackle." After learning some of the Couple Communication skills, the man's confidence in both his ability to communicate painful information and in their ability as a couple to deal with difficult issues gave him the security to risk coming forth with the truth: "It was one of the most humiliating and painful things I've ever done. But our level of trust and intimacy is deeper because of it. With God's help and some practical tools, we came to the river . . . and crossed it."

Question 3
What are your foci for counseling?

One of the best-known mottos of many discipleship programs is "Give me a fish, and I'll eat for a day; teach me to fish, and I'll eat for a lifetime." Couple Communication is a program that teaches people how to "fish." Its purpose is to build satisfying relationships by increasing interpersonal competence. This is achieved by learning practical conceptual frameworks (insight), communication skills, and interactional processes. Learning occurs around real-life issues with feedback and coaching (from both the instructor and other participants) on their interaction.

The Scriptures are filled with admonishments to speak truth and listen respectfully. The Couple Communication program and the workbook *Talking and Listening Together* operationalize this guidance with behavioral skills. While the text does not reference specific Scriptures, biblical teachers freely integrate Scripture with the program. It is not uncommon for participants to tell us how much the program concepts and skills have helped them translate their faith into everyday practice, particularly in stressful situations at home and work.

Question 4
How is your marriage counseling conducted?

The program begins with a maxi-contracting session. Either in person or by telephone, the instructor uses an informational brochure on the program to contract with each couple for participation. The maxi-contract assures that both partners understand the goals and nature of the program and that both partners want to participate. Since the program is for couples, both partners must be willing to participate. While the maxi-contract only takes about ten to fifteen minutes, on the average, this initial contact is worth a session in itself. Any difficulty such as poor attendance, low involvement, or unfulfilled expectations during the program can usually be traced easily to a poor or nonexistent maxi-contract. Whether the program is taught with up to twelve couples as an enrichment event or integrated into conjoint marriage counseling, having a treatment plan that establishes a maxi-contract is essential.

Couples learn to create mini-contracts during the program. Mini-contracting precedes any group activity in which the couples would be discussing an issue in front of and receiving feedback from other couple participants. The mini-contract puts each couple in charge of their own disclosure and learning by deciding (a) if they want to participate in a particular exercise, (b) which issue to talk about that would be appropriate in the context while respecting their privacy and individual/couple boundaries, and (c) whether they want feedback on their skill usage from other participants and the instructor. The mini-contract enhances the partners' sense of agency—being able to choose what, when, where, and how to communicate.

The group format is spread over four two-hour sessions (typically within four weeks). The conjoint format teaches the program material in six fifty-minute sessions. Methodologically, all group and conjoint sessions are built around five activities.

1. Assessments and action plans. Preprogram and postprogram skill assessments and session action plans are contained in each partner's *Talking and Listening Together* workbook.
2. Brief presentations of conceptual frameworks (maps) and skills.
3. Skill and process demonstrations. Participants are able to see on "live" videos or prerecorded programs the skills and processes modeled around real issues. When instructor-couples teach the program using their own current issues, the demonstrations add a particularly personal and powerful dimension to the program.
4. Skill and process practice. A major portion of each session is devoted to actual skill practice and experiential learning around real issues.

5. Transfer of learning. The program is best taught with time between sessions (a week or so) in order for partners to apply the skills, day-to-day, together.

A unique feature of Couple Communication is the use of skill mats (one for talking and another for listening) for accelerated learning. These thirty-inch-square canvas floor mats are printed with communication skill frameworks on them. As partners actually step about on the mats, the tools (a) structure who talks and who listens; (b) help partners delimit and focus on a single issue; (c) slow down interaction; (d) facilitate clear, direct, and congruent talking; (e) access deeper and richer information; (f) reduce defensive listening; (g) substitute concrete constructive skills (options) for destructive habits; and (h) integrate the sensate, cognitive, affective, conative, and behavioral dimensions of interaction. The mats also leverage learning. Around a large room, a number of couples can work simultaneously practicing skills and receiving feedback and coaching. Couples use the skills mats during each session and between sessions for skill practice. Then they retain them for continued use, skill review, and reinforcement.

Session 1, in the group format, focuses on caring about oneself because effective communication flows out of self-awareness and skill in communicating that self-awareness. The session introduces (a) the Awareness Wheel, which is a map for understanding issues; (b) Self-talk, which is a process of recognizing and expanding personal awareness; and (c) six talking skills for expressing the self more clearly. Theoretically, this first session focuses on individuation—being able to acknowledge, accept, and congruently act on all parts of experience—sensory data, thoughts, feelings, wants, and behaviors.

Session 2 focuses on caring about one's partner because relationships grow with attentive listening and accurate understanding. The session teaches five listening skills and the use of the Listening Cycle, a process for ensuring complete information and accurate understanding of each partner's concern. Theoretically, this second session emphasizes differentiation—the capacity to understand and affirm the partner while maintaining separateness.

Session 3 focuses on resolving conflicts because the manner in which partners handle conflicts determines the quality of their resolutions and their satisfaction with the relationship. During the session, the partners identify their typical patterns for handling conflicts, learn ways to set comfortable procedures for managing conflicts, and practice an eight-step collaborative conflict-resolving process, called *mapping issues*. Theoretically, this session operationalizes collaboration.

The last group session (session 4) presents styles of communication because partners respond as much to how something is said as to what is said. Participants learn the characteristics of four distinct styles of talking and listening, the positive and negative impacts of each style, and the fit between the styles and all the Couple Communication concepts and skills taught in the program. Theoretically, style is an index of a couple's relationship. How partners talk reflects how they relate and their level of satisfaction.

Question 5
How do you deal with a few of the common marital problems?

While we were writing this chapter, one of our students in the doctor of ministry program at Denver Seminary phoned. He is involved in a church ministry on the East Coast. With enthusiasm that was hard for him to control, he told about a couple he had seen for three sessions. The wife was fed up with her husband's inability or unwillingness to open up and talk about issues. The husband was frustrated by his wife's pressure to communicate about things that were not natural for him to talk about. The counselor thought he was at an impasse.

As almost a "last gasp" effort, the counselor decided that rather than have the couple continue to do what had not worked for over twenty years, he would contract with them to learn Couple Communication—some new ways of communicating. They both agreed. To the counselor's (and the wife's) amazement, the husband began to open up as never before when he got on the "feelings" section of the Awareness Wheel mat. The minister concluded, "That simple little tool proved to be the turning point in our counseling and in their marriage relationship." The skills mats are particularly useful in restructuring asymmetrical relationships, as well as pursuing or withdrawing relationship patterns such as the one our student encountered.

Although it may sound grandiose, we have not seen an issue—topical, personal, or relational—that cannot be more effectively processed by a couple using the six talking and five listening skills taught in Couple Communication. The program can be used effectively in churches as enrichment or in counseling as part of a treatment plan.

Tasks 1 and 2
Respond to the case study by telling precisely how you might typically treat it, in how many sessions, in what order, and with what responses by the clients throughout counseling. One restriction: Assume that between the third and fourth counseling sessions with you—regardless of what had gone on during the previous session—the couple had a major argument and come to the fourth session in some crisis.

Create a dialogue between the counselor and the couple (or one spouse, if you prefer) showing how you might deal with communication difficulties.

Contracting Session

The goals of the session are to define the problem, assess individual and couple strengths, consider solutions, create hope, build positive expectancies, establish a commitment for change, and begin the change process. (The issues of treatment and a typical dialogue intertwine, and they are dealt with together in this section.) From the first interview with Art and Pam, it was clear that there were myriad issues that could be addressed. After fourteen years of marriage, they had become married singles. They presented as two people who were unhappy with themselves and each other. I found the addressable issues to include intrapersonal development, their families of origin, a stagnant relationship, negative feelings, unhealthy anger, blame, depression, a poor sexual relationship, infertility, an affair, a lack of forgiveness, personal and professional identities, and limited conflict-resolution skills, to name but a few. (Though this chapter is written by two authors-counselors, only one counselor would typically see Art and Pam. Accordingly, in this response to the case study and in the simulated dialogues, we will refer to the counselor as "I.")

One of the most important questions of the first session is where to start. What a couple wants and what a therapist thinks they need can be two different things. While it is important to focus on the problems, it is equally important to determine what a successful outcome will look like through their eyes. Toward the end of the session, I asked, "If counseling is successful, what will be different about your relationship?" They both answered, "We will get along better."

I followed up the couple's response with, "When you are getting along better, what will you be doing that is different from what you have been doing?" This time their response took a bit longer. Pam was the first to answer: "We won't fight as much." Art nodded in agreement.

"That sounds like a reasonable goal," I replied. "If you do less fighting, what will you be doing more of?" Now there was an even longer pause. While it is common for couples to define progress by doing less of something, I have found it is of limited value to define progress by negation, by doing less of something or by eliminating some behavior. In such cases, therapy is still problem focused rather than solution focused. Progress is made by moving toward something rather than away from something. "If our work here is successful," Art stated, "we will be communicating and understanding each other more, and fighting less." This was a step toward a more concrete and positive goal.

Early on in the therapy process, it is helpful to get a sense of how a couple would rate their marriage and rate their commitment to making the marriage work. The first piece of information helps the therapist assess their current level of satisfaction, and it also serves as a baseline by which to measure improvement. The second piece of information helps determine the level of commitment. The easiest way to measure these variables is to use a scaling question. I asked Art and Pam, "On a scale from one to ten, with one being the pits and ten being ecstasy, how happy are you in your marriage?" They both looked at each other and then at the floor. Finally Pam said, "I think I would give it a two or a three." I could tell by the look on Art's face that he was surprised by her response. Finally, he replied, "I think I would give it a four or a five." Pam immediately responded by saying, "You've got to be kidding!"

The next step was to assess the couple's degree of commitment to making the marriage work. They appeared motivated to resolve their marital difficulties, and both stated their firm belief in the permanence of marriage. However, they were stuck in a deep relational rut. I asked them, "On a scale from one to ten, with one being you couldn't care less and ten being you are willing to do whatever it takes to make your marriage work, how would you rate your own commitment?" Art immediately responded with, "At least an eight or a nine." This time Pam smiled and said, "You've surprised me again. But it's a pleasant surprise." She continued, "That's what I would say, an eight or a nine."

At this point, I knew Art and Pam had a troubled marriage. Neither was very happy in it. At the same time they both had a strong commitment to making it work. So where would we start? Obviously, there were many things they needed to talk about, but they did not have the tools. They spoke the same language but they did not communicate.

Given Art and Pam's wide range of problems, stated goals, and available resources, I decided the best place for them to begin might be in the area of communication. At the outset of working with a couple, I attempt to define a goal that has an almost 100 percent probability of success, one that will help address the problem, give the couple a success, strengthen their relationship, and generalize to other relational areas. The strength of this approach is clear: as the couple develops essential skills and adds tools to their "relational toolbox," their basic issues are worked on, and simultaneously the foundation for ongoing growth is laid.

I talked with Art and Pam about the importance of communication, since neither of them had grown up in a home where healthy communication or conflict-resolution skills were modeled. Then I used the Couple Communication 1 brochure to introduce Pam and Art to the program. We discussed Couple Communication's background (development and research foundation); content (concepts and skills); formats (group or conjoint sessions); methods (the coaching and practicing of skills while processing their real issues); materials (the Couple Packet, which includes workbooks, skill mats, and pocket cards); and benefits to them. I also talked about the importance of each partner's willingness to (a) take the preprogram skill assessment to set individual learning goals and the post-program skill assessment to measure progress; (b) read sections in the workbook; (c) practice skills and complete assignments between sessions (the changes that take place between our sessions are often the most important ones); and (d) participate fully in learning the material for oneself and for each other.

Pam and Art each had some questions that represented no resistance and were easily clarified. They also decided to participate conjointly rather than in a group—they wanted the individualized coaching and privacy. The couple established a maxi-contact to spend six sessions learning communication and conflict-resolution concepts and skills while they worked through their real issues. I gave Art and Pam a Couple Packet and the following assignment: to complete the preprogram skill assessment and goal setting and to read the first chapter in their workbooks *(Talking and Listening Together)*. When they had no further questions, I closed the session in prayer.

Session 1

The session began with a brief review of Art and Pam's learning goals, based on their self-scored pre-assessments. Art's goals were fewer spiteful, undercutting remarks; less giving in to Pam's decisions; more acknowledgment of Pam's wants and desires; more sharing of feelings; and less arguing and fighting. Pam's goals were less speaking for Art; less forcing decisions on Art; more disclosure of her own wants and desires; more resolving issues by building agreements collaboratively; and more pleasant, fun conversations. I identified the six talking skills and related them to each partner's learning goals.

I then used the Awareness Wheel (chap. 1 in the workbook) to demonstrate how an individual can take care of oneself. As an exercise for learning to use the wheel, each partner picks an individual (nonrelational) issue to process using the skills mat. This tool helps partners organize their thinking, and it prompts more clear and complete disclosure. Art's issue was "pressure at work," and Pam's was "finding a part-time job." Both partners processed their issues without questions or advice from the other. I helped each partner accurately and kinesthetically match awareness and words with the corresponding zone on the Awareness Wheel.

In order for Art and Pam to prepare at home for the next session, I asked them to (a) use the Awareness Wheel skills mat to do one or two exercises at the end of chapter 1 in the workbook; (b) read "Caring About Our Partner: Listening" in the workbook; (c) look up Scripture references, listed on a one-page handout, that deal with communication and listening; and (d) pray.

Session 2

I introduced to Art and Pam five listening skills and the Listening Cycle. Then I requested they each use the listening skills mat to practice listening to an issue of their partner's choosing. At this point, the goal was to exercise listening skills to achieve understanding, not necessarily agreement or solution. In particular, Art practiced the skill of "acknowledging," and Pam, the skill of "inviting." Once again, I assigned homework: (a) discuss an issue with one partner on the Awareness Wheel skills mat and the other on the Listening Cycle skills mat, each partner taking a turn on each mat; (b) read "Resolving Conflicts: Mapping Issues" in the workbook; and (c) talk about the potential value of conflict and start the reframing of conflict as having potential for intimacy.

Session 3

When Art and Pam walked into my office, they did not need to tell me what had happened. Although I didn't know the details, it was obvious as they sat on opposite ends of the couch that they were stuck in a conflict. When I asked, "What's gone better the past week?" Art's immediate reply was, "Nothing!"

"What can you tell me about 'nothing'?" I asked.

"Well," Pam started, "as I look back, it really was about nothing. That's what's so frustrating. Most of the time, after the fireworks have gone off, we both decide that the issue wasn't that big a deal."

Identify crisis issue. Pam told me that she had opened up the credit-card statement and discovered over two hundred dollars in charges of which she had not been aware. Pam said, "We've agreed that we wouldn't charge more than seventy-five dollars without discussing it together."

Art jumped in, "I had just walked in the door. It had been a frustrating and draining day at work, and as soon as I walk in, she hits me with, 'What in the world did you spend this money on?'" He continued, "After Pam asked me to account for my spending, it didn't take us long to move from question and answer to raised voices, shouting, accusations of 'you always' and 'you never,' and inevitably I stomped out with Pam in hot pursuit."

"From what you've told me, this sounds like a common pattern," I observed.

Both Art and Pam agreed. For years they had experienced frustrating and futile fights over similar issues. They would become so focused on the content of the issue that they had never noticed the reoccurring process that kept them stuck. Even though it had never worked, they had stayed in a rut of responding in the same ineffective way. They were discouraged and felt hopeless about their marriage ever changing.

Contract to work through the issue. I asked the couple if they would be willing to put the skills mats on the floor and let me coach them as they worked through the credit-card issue. Both were willing. We laid the skills mats for talking and listening on the floor, and without elaborating, I began to walk them through the Mapping-an-Issue process.

To interrupt their typical pattern of Pam's pursuing and Art's with-drawing, I invited, "Art, would you begin talking first?"

Understand the issue completely. Art stepped onto the *thinking* zone first and said, "I don't think you trust me."

Pam immediately said, "I do, too."

I said, "Pam, instead of reacting, *invite* Art to say more."

She said, "Art, tell me more."

Art proceeded, "Very often you force me to—"

I interrupted, "Try *speaking for self,* Art."

He continued, "Often I let [*action*] myself be forced into agreeing with something I don't really buy into. And then when I deviate from your solution, I get clobbered—like the credit-card incident [*data*]. I *think* that if you really trusted me, I could act more freely without being grilled and second-guessed frequently. I resent it [*feeling*] when I think you distrust me and *feel* angry having to answer to you about so many things I think are insignificant."

I prompted Pam, "*Summarize* what Art just said, and *invite* him to say more." She did.

Art said, "That's it."

The couple exchanged mats. Pam stepped onto the *feeling* zone and said, "It really scares me when I *think* things are getting out of control." She began to cry.

Art, *acknowledging* Pam's feelings, said, "My spending frightens you."

She sobbed, "Yes." There was a long but comfortable silence. Then Pam went to the past—to her childhood—and began stepping around the zones of the Awareness Wheel recalling events [*data*], *thoughts,* and *feelings* she had as a small girl growing up with the insecurities of a father who spent money foolishly and was always broke. Pam shifted back into the present and said to Art, "I know you don't handle money like my dad does, but I still get scared."

Art quietly *invited,* "Anything else?"

Pam stepped onto the *wants* zone and said, "I *want for me* not to worry about our finances. And I *want for you* not to have me on your back about every dime you spend."

103

Identify wants. I asked Art, "Do you have any wants you wish to express?"

Art responded, "Yes," and stepped onto the *wants* zone of the Awareness Wheel as Pam moved back onto the listening mat. He said, "I want you to trust my judgment with money, Pam. I'd like the freedom to buy things once in a while without getting your okay." Then he looked down at the *wants for other* zone and after a long pause continued, "I don't often think about your wants, Pam, and what I *want for you.*" Then he stepped across the mat and said, "I *feel* embarrassed that I don't know what I want for you."

I *invited* Art, "Keep going."

He said, "That's it."

Then I said, "Art, recall what Pam has just told about the story of her growing up, and see if there is anything you could want for her from what you heard her saying."

He promptly stepped back onto the *wants for other* zone, looked at Pam, and said, "I want for you to feel comfortable with our finances."

Pam smiled.

Generate options. I said, "I wonder if you would each brainstorm some things you could do to put your awareness into action. Pam?"

Pam responded, "I guess I could tell Art when I feel anxious about our finances rather than just jump on him for buying something." She also suggested, "I could say nothing, but that would be hard to do."

Art said, "I will support your looking for part-time work, Pam, if that would give you a better sense of personal financial freedom and security."

Pam said, "I like that idea."

Choose actions. After some additional discussion, I asked, "Would you each step on the *future action* zone and say what you will be willing to do in relation to the issue of trust and spending?"

Art said, "Pam, I will support you in looking for part-time work."

Pam said, "I will tell you, Art, when I am feeling anxious about finances, without blaming you for my anxiety."

Test the action plans. To test the couple's action plans, I asked, "Are there any dangling data, thoughts, feelings, or wants related to the issue that either of you wants to bring up?"

Both answered at once, "No," and they looked congruent in saying so.

After Art and Pam had used the mats to communicate about the crisis issue, there was little time remaining in the session. However, in order to link the process I had just taken them through with the content of their issue, I asked them to turn in their workbooks to chapter 3, "Resolving Conflicts: Mapping Issues," and to also take out their pocket cards for Mapping-an-Issue. The card listed eight steps.

1. Identify and define the issue.
2. Contract to work through the issue.
3. Understand the issue completely.
4. Identify wants.
5. Generate options.
6. Choose actions.
7. Test the action plan.
8. Evaluate the outcome.

Seeing the listed steps helped Art and Pam move beyond the content of their conflict to a realization of a potential underlying process that they could use to resolve issues.

I assigned two tasks for homework: (a) review "Resolving Conflicts: Mapping Issues" in the workbook and (b) use the skills mats to map an issue on their own.

Session 4

This session began with a discussion of conflict resolution in terms of processes, outcomes, and patterns. (Normally we would have covered this material in session 3, but the intensity of the credit-card issue necessitated flexibility in covering course material.) The processes of avoiding, persuading, floating, compromising, and collaborating typically lead to different outcomes, independent of the content of the issue. After the couple identified and discussed their typical patterns (Pam persuades and Art avoids), the two chose a conflict to map—using the skill mats with my coaching.

The issue chosen was adoption of a child. Though the couple underwent fertility testing and Art was discovered to be functionally sterile, they had never further discussed the issue of having children. Both thought discussing adoption would provide them with the opportunity to practice talking and listening skills as they worked through a problem-solving process collaboratively. The session was very enlightening to both of them in terms of sharing thoughts, feelings, and wants. Neither person was ready to commit to a future action—the next step—but they agreed that just opening the discussion was a good first step.

I assigned one task for homework: read "Choosing Communication Styles: Ways of Talking and Listening" in the workbook.

Session 5

When Pam and Art entered my office for the fifth session, there was an immediate nonverbal difference in the air. They seemed freer and lighter. I could not help but inquire about the difference.

Art began talking. On Sunday the minister had preached a powerful sermon on forgiveness. At the end, the pastor encouraged folks to inventory their own lives and confront their own issues of forgiveness. While Art and Pam both *claimed* that Art's one-night affair with a coworker had been forgiven and forgotten, Art really did not believe that was true, thinking more realistically that he had tried to avoid the issue and that Pam had been too quick to forgive.

That afternoon, feeling more comfortable and confident (skilled) in his ability to communicate with Pam, Art had asked her if she would be willing to talk about the affair again. Pam was willing. Art had then said he did not want to stand on the skill mats to talk about the issue, but wanted to have the mats nearby on the floor to prompt a constructive discussion. The two used the mapping structure to talk openly and honestly about the event and the impact it had had on each of their lives and their relationship. The outcome of the discussion was honest accountability and forgiveness.

In telling about their encounter, both Art and Pam expressed some guilt at not having conducted the discussion in my counseling office. I told them that I was delighted that I had not been there. My job was, in fact, to help them gain the skills and confidence to work through complicated and potentially loaded issues on their own, to their own mutual satisfaction. This is what the Couple Communication program is all about—helping couples become their own best problem solvers. They seemed relieved that they had not hurt me in some way by going ahead with this serious discussion on their own. Their story was a good lead into discussing styles of communication and how, until recently, their repertoire had been limited and limiting.

I assigned two tasks for homework: (a) read "Choosing Communication Styles on 'Mixed Messages'" in the workbook and (b) complete the postprogram questionnaire (assessment) of their skill learning and goal attainment.

Session 6

We discussed the homework assignment, Choosing Communication Styles on "Mixed Messages." Both partners had decided they wanted to send more straight messages and listen more attentively. Pam said she overused "control" talk and began practicing more open questions and "search" talk. Art said he was often indirect and slipped into "spite" talk (cynicism, foot-dragging, complaining, whining, pouting, ignoring, or withholding affection and information). Using the Awareness Wheel helped him identify his feelings and wants and express them congruently.

To reinforce the impact of style, I had the partners role-play an issue. We started with each partner's preferred style and then talked about it. Art and Pam both moved to "straight" talk and discussed that, too. Finally, we summarized the counseling experience and discussed termination.

The postprogram assessment helped Art and Pam in two ways. It helped them to identify some of the specific gains they had made in their marriage relationship. They saw that they not only had gained some valuable insights, but also had developed some simple, practical, and powerful new tools to make their communication more positive and productive.

At the end of our last session, Art turned to me and said, "I've been surprised how something so simple as the Awareness Wheel has made such a difference in the way we communicate." As Pam nodded in agreement she added, "I know that we will still have our disagreements, but now I also know that we have the tools to grow through them."

References

Hoff, L., and W. R. Miller. 1981. *Marriage enrichment philosophy, process, and program.* Bowie, Md.: Robert J. Brady.

Miller, S., P. Miller, E. W. Nunnally, and D. B. Wackman. 1992. *Couple Communication instructor manual.* Littleton, Colo.: Interpersonal Communication Programs.

Wampler, K. S. 1990. An update of research on the Couple Communication program. *Family Science Review* 3, no. 1:21–40.

Additional Resources

For brochures and a catalog about the Couple Communication program—couple or instructor materials, training, and certification—or other programs and materials for individuals and teams, call 800-328-5099 or write to Interpersonal Communication Programs, Inc., 7201 South Broadway, Suite #11, Littleton, Colorado 80122.

Oliver, G. J. 1993. *Masculinity at the crossroads.* Chicago: Moody.

———.1993. *Real men have feelings, too.* Chicago: Moody.

Oliver, G. J., and H. N. Wright. 1995. *Good women get angry: A woman's guide to handling anger, depression, anxiety, and stress.* Ann Arbor: Servant.

Wright, H. N., and G. J. Oliver. 1994. *How to change your spouse (without ruining your marriage).* Ann Arbor: Servant.

Relationship Development

Les Parrott III and Leslie Parrott

Question 1
What are the basics of your theory of marriage counseling? In your description, include your view of the typical cause(s) of marital problems and the typical goals of counseling.

The primary emphasis of our work is premarital, neomarital, and early-marriage counseling. As codirectors of the Center for Relationship Development at Seattle Pacific University, we believe deeply in the impact of preventive interventions on the permanence, intimacy, and satisfaction of marriage. Research has underscored a tendency for minor problems in marriage to escalate into major rifts if they are not addressed promptly. Marcia Lasswell (1985) reports that half of all serious marital problems develop in the first two years of marriage. Our experiences in marriage and family therapy have confirmed this prognosis and shaped our emphasis on treating marriages in their early phases. As Christians, our perspective on marriage counseling is grounded in the belief that marriages characterized by permanence, intimacy, and oneness are achieved in full measure only within the context of a vital faith in Christ. Without a deep dependency on Christ as the ultimate source of security and significance, the marriage relationship cannot support a commitment of ministry to the deepest needs—body and soul—of each partner (Les Parrott 1994).

Family-Systems Theory

Our approach to marriage counseling has been fundamentally shaped by family-systems theory as presented by Murray Bowen (1978) in his seminal work, *Family Therapy in Clinical Practice*. It has also been profoundly influenced by the contributions of one of Bowen's former students, namely, Edwin Friedman (1985), who has been a pioneer in applying systems theory to religious congregations and families within the church. Others who have significantly influenced our approach to marriage therapy are Betty Carter and Monica McGoldrick (1989), systems therapists who emphasize the importance of the family life cycle in marital therapy.

As practitioners in an academic setting, we also place a high value on the contribution of research to the prevention and repair of marriage problems. Our counseling model continues to be reshaped by such recent work as Howard Markman's and Scott Stanley's Prevention and Relationship Enhancement Program (PREP) and Christian PREP (Markman et al. 1991), John Gottman's (1994) ongoing research at the University of Washington on conflict in relationships, and David Olson's and his associates' PREPARE/ENRICH premarital/marital assessment tool (Olson, Fourier, and Druckman 1987).

Our therapeutic model views the couple in the context of the intergenerational family system. Systemic dynamics flowing through the extended family transfer relationship and communication patterns (myths, secrets, and legacies) into the marital system. In addition, as the couple moves through the developmental passages of the life cycle (marriage, birth, family, empty nest, retirement, and death), these transitions dynamically impact the extended family system. Symptoms or problems may occur in healthy marriages when there is extraordinary developmental stress (e.g., untimely death, chronic illness, birth of a handicapped child). However, even minor developmental stressors can cause problems for a family that is coping with dysfunctional extended-family relationship dynamics (Carter and McGoldrick 1989).

"Relationship patterns in families," states Michael Kerr, "are all variations of a basic theme: anxiety generated by people's difficulty thinking, feeling, and acting for themselves when closely involved with others, especially during periods of heightened stress. The patterns in which anxiety plays out in families are knowable, finite in number, and universal" (1992, p. x). There are several relational patterns that are established by marriage partners (and families) to manage anxiety: (a) conflict, (b) distance (which paradoxically intensifies feelings over time), (c) over-functioning-underfunctioning reciprocity (one partner becomes dysfunctional), and (d) triangulating.

From our family-systems perspective, there are three significant measures of marital health: (a) the marriage relationship (how much conflict and distance is present); (b) the physical and emotional health of each marriage partner, including evidence of an overfunctioning-underfunctioning reciprocity; and (c) the emotional and physical health of each of the children, including relationships with each of the parents and with the siblings that might indicate the presence of entrenched relational triangles. Marriages are considered to be healthy to the extent that the entire family system is symptom free. It is impossible to measure the health of a marriage without an understanding of the entire nuclear family. From a family-systems perspective, difficulties in marriage have less to do with the differences between marriage partners than with what is causing the differences to be highlighted at the present time (Friedman 1985).

Self-Differentiation

It is our belief, based on systems thinking, that curative work in the context of marriage therapy allows a couple to achieve authentic intimacy, rather than live in fusion or disengagement. Such achievement requires that each partner mature in his or her level of self-differentiation, which according to Bowen, is the ability to have well-thought-out life values, principles, and convictions and to hold onto them in the face of anxiety and pressure for conformity and togetherness. Thus, self-differentiation is the capacity to maintain relationships based on emotional separateness, equality, and openness and is manifest in the person who is able to say, "This is who I am, what I believe, what I stand for, and what I will do or will not do in a given situation." Bowen states: "A more differentiated person can participate freely in the emotional sphere without the fear of becoming too fused with others. He or she also is free to shift to calm, logical reasoning for decisions that govern life. A well differentiated person is not changed by coercion or pressure, or to gain approval, or enhance one's stand with others" (Bowen 1971, in Gilbert 1992, 193–94). This concept should not be confused with autonomy or narcissism. Differentiation includes the capacity to maintain a nonanxious presence in the midst of anxious systems while taking full personal responsibility for one's emotional well-being (Friedman 1985).

Roberta Gilbert (1992) suggests the following characteristics in relationships characterized by self-differentiation: (a) emotional calm (a nonanxious presence), (b) intellectual objectivity (the ability to observe self in a relationship pattern and make changes without expectations of the other), (c) maintenance of one-to-one relationships with one's spouse and the individuals in one's extended family, (d) during conflict, a view of others as anxious or fearful (rather than malicious or manipulative), (e) the ability not to react in kind to anger or anxiety of others, (f) the ability to make choices or define positions that may jeopardize love, approval, acceptance, and nurturing, (g) a focus more on personal responsibility than on the behavior of others in the relationship, and (h) calm and thoughtful decision making.

From a Christian perspective, self-differentiation in marriage reflects a deep dependency on Christ for the fulfillment of personal needs (rather than a manipulative attempt to have the partner meet personal needs) and a choice to engage in behavior in the relationship that reflects the love and value Christ places on each spouse.

When individuals in a marriage relationship are undifferentiated, they get caught up in a pattern of emotional reactivity that incorporates the patterns of conflict, distance, cutoff, overfunctioning-underfunctioning reciprocity, and triangulating rather than true intimacy. The goal of marriage counseling is to move the couple further up on the self-differentiation scale, resulting in a more authentic connection.

The role of the family of origin is central to marriage counseling from our perspective. In other words, the marital dyad cannot be considered in isolation from the extended families of origin of both partners. Friedman eloquently states, "The position we occupy in our families of origin is the only thing we can never share or give to another while we are still alive. It is the source of our uniqueness, and hence, the basic parameter for our emotional potential as well as our difficulties. . . . The more we understand that position, therefore, and the more we can learn to occupy it with grace and 'savvy,' rather than fleeing from it or unwittingly allowing it to program our destiny, the more perfectly we can function in any other area of our life" (1985, 34).

Spiritual Growth

Our approach to marriage counseling from a Christian perspective demands much of us as therapists. It requires us to be individuals who have listened to Scripture and who have wrestled with its application in our own relational challenges. As counselors, we must model our own self-differentiation, being willing and able to answer forthrightly any questions clients may ask about our values and doctrinal beliefs (Worthington 1989). In family-systems therapy, although the big picture is the ultimate health of the marriage, the focus is not on the marital problem to be solved, but on the development and maturity of each marriage partner (resulting in a better relational system). This focus on the personal development of a system of beliefs, values, and guiding life principles, with the resultant focus on living those out within the most demanding of relationships, is a deeply spiritual task. Admittedly, Bowen's theory in its purist form is tied to an evolutionary philosophy and does not support the existence of absolute truth (Worthington 1989, 336–37). However, it is possible to use Bowen's theory without adopting his philosophical assumptions. Friedman, for instance, has applied systems theory to the process of spiritual conversion (1985). Because our work is conducted in a Christian context, most of our clients pursue spiritual growth and are strengthened in accomplishing spiritual growth within the framework of their faith in Christ.

The central idea that we would like troubled spouses to learn from counseling is the paradox at the heart of relational process: To work on a relationship, one must work on oneself. In order to be less distant, each marriage partner must develop stronger, healthier personal boundaries.

Question 2
For what kind of people is your approach most appropriate?

The family-systems counseling approach is appropriate for premarital couples, married couples, and families operating with a broad range of functional-dysfunctional symptoms. The preventive model Saving Your Marriage Before It Starts (SYMBIS), described in Question 4, is designed for premarital and early married couples who are comfortable operating within a Christian context (Les Parrott and Leslie Parrott 1995). Both the SYMBIS program and the family-systems approach are equally effective when used by mental-health professionals and pastoral counselors. We consider the involvement of a network of support (marriage mentor couples) to be a crucial element in the long-term impact of the counseling and educational interventions.

Question 3
What are your foci for counseling?

Teaching Systems Thinking

Through the creation of a family genogram (a type of multi-generational family tree that records family patterns and relationship information) for each of the partners, the emphasis shifts from a direct focus on the relationship to an indirect focus on the issues that may emerge with the joining of two family systems. Relational patterns (conflicts, cutoffs, distance, enmeshment, and triangles) are explored with ramifications for the couple's relationship. Important life-cycle issues are explored with an emphasis on insight for future transitions that are likely to induce a high level of anxiety and disruption for the couple and the extended family.

Systems thinking is also underscored through an exploration of the sibling position of each partner and the resultant impact of those roles on the marital relationship. Research indicates that marital stability is affected by the sibling position of each spouse (Toman 1976). Partners who can anticipate the impact of their sibling position on their own role in the relationship are better equipped for marriage.

Defining "I" Positions

With the goal of increased self-differentiation, we seek to facilitate the counseling process with opportunities for each partner to further define himself or herself within the relational system. Issues that involve high levels of anxiety and emotional reactivity for the couple are seen as opportunities for further self-differentiation within the extended family and within the marital dyad. The counselor simply works to help each partner take clear "I" positions while the other partner practices active listening (reflecting emotion and clarifying content). In our experience, marriage conflict is largely a fight to be heard and understood (even when the differences cause anxiety) rather than a problem to be resolved.

Using Play and Paradox

Strategic interventions within the marital system and the extended family system often incorporate an element of playfulness (not a clever sense of humor, but a creative and flexible relationship stance). Because the presence of chronic anxiety is linked to an attitude of seriousness (concentrated focus, inflexibility, intensity of effort), the relational impact of playfulness often, paradoxically, produces change (Friedman 1985). We encourage the partners to think creatively about a response that might be "out of character" for them. This process is often aided by an exercise that identifies the controlling strategies of each partner (e.g., pleasing, teaching, blaming, avoiding, protecting), and identifies one action each can take that might be the *opposite*. Another option is to have them take their usual stance in the relationship, but exaggerate it to a melodramatic level. This ability to play out the caricature of their role allows for a creative distance from it and introduces a playful element in the interactions. Both of these paradoxical interventions frequently open up the system and allow growth and change to occur.

Using Rites of Passage and Rituals

From a systems perspective, the wedding ceremony provides an opportunity to intervene in the emotional processes of the family with a positive, differentiating impact on the couple that allows them to "leave and cleave" (see Gen. 2:24). Family attitudes and myths about marriage filter down from generation to generation, shaping a unique experience of this life-cycle transition for the couple. The family life-cycle does not always evolve smoothly and methodically, but often is "rather uneven, sometimes halting, sometimes rapid . . . like a train with a steam engine pumping its way up hill, straining for the top, running smoothly for a while once it reaches a plateau, and racing down the other side" (Koman and Stechler 1985, 7). The wedding ceremony and resultant marriage can be likened to a racing train for some families while for others it is a slow engine struggling uphill. Carter and McGoldrick (1989) identify two common family patterns: (a) marriage is viewed as such an enormous task that it can never be sufficiently prepared for and (b) marriage is seen as the fulfillment of all needs, regardless of all other aspects of life.

As family tensions arise (disapproving in-laws, overinvolved or underinvolved family members), the couple can be coached to be attentive to the family process rather than to the content of the issues raised. Focusing on family process will allow the transitional family relationships to avoid (and perhaps resolve) relational distancing, cutoffs, and triangles that can interfere with the couple's ability to connect with each other.

Question 4
How is your marriage counseling conducted?

In the Center for Relationship Development, our intervention model begins with an emphasis on insight through an educational experience. This two-day workshop, entitled "Saving Your Marriage Before It Starts" (SYMBIS), addresses (a) marital myths, (b) marital conflict, (c) gender differences and sexuality in marriage, (d) money management, and (e) marriage as a covenantal relationship. The goal of this two-day seminar is twofold: (a) preventing an escalation in anxiety in the newly married couple by demythifying early marriage and (b) raising the level of self-efficacy of each partner to impact the marriage relationship positively. Following this two-day event, couples engage in a year-long relationship with a marriage mentor couple. Mentoring allows for timely connection with a mature and healthy couple for a minimum of three times: at three months, at seven months, and at the completion of the first year. These activities are also designed as preventive interventions that may short-circuit anxiety by normalizing the experiences of early marriage (as they connect through often humorous stories and experiences of the mentor couple) and by intervening in detrimental patterns before they become entrenched ways of relating.

Premarital counseling is conducted from the family-systems approach, which is particularly applicable at this significant life-cycle transition characterized by a flux in family relationships. Rather than focusing directly on the relationship of the couple, we facilitate a guided exploration of the extended family through the use of a family genogram for each partner. This is useful as an indicator of future rough waters for the couple, as a tool for separating from parents more easily, and as a way to explore the relationship with a depth not possible when the focus is directed only on the couple. Each couple who seeks premarital counseling is required to make a commitment to an agreed-upon number of postmarital sessions during the first year of marriage.

Question 5
How do you deal with a few of the common marital problems?

Fusion versus Intimacy

In *Finding the Love of Your Life*, Neal Clark Warren (1992) identifies a lack of intimacy as the number one enemy of marriage. He goes on to say that if two people do not know each other deeply, they can never become what the Bible calls "one flesh" (Gen. 2:24). They will never bond. "Without intimacy," he says, "they will be isolated and alone—even while living under the same roof" (Warren 1992, 103). The fulfillment of love hinges on the closeness, sharing, communication, honesty, and support in intimacy. As one heart given in exchange for another, marriage is designed to provide the deepest and most radical expression of intimacy. The path to intimacy, however, is often completely misunderstood. As couples attempt to achieve intimacy, they so often confuse the work of forming an intimate relationship with their own need for the relationship to complete them, becoming overly dependent on their partner for their own identity and esteem.

This type of relational fusion (masquerading as intimacy) leads to a high level of relational stress. In *Letters to a Young Poet*, Rainer

Maria Rilke states, "Love is at first not anything that means merging, giving over, and uniting with another (for that would a union be of something unclarified and unfinished, still subordinate?); it is a high inducement to the individual to ripen . . . it is a great exacting claim" (1954, 54). The type of union struck between two partners in fusion fosters an unhealthy emotional climate. When either of the fused partners is dissatisfied (angry, depressed, or stuck), blame is placed on the other. When anxiety and stress become intense, couples in fusion tend to define their problems solely within the relationship. As the couple becomes more entrenched in relational fusion over time, the more the emotions of each spouse are seen as the result of the other, causing the couple's communication to become inflexible, constricted, and emotionally charged (Carter and McGoldrick 1989). Fusion in relationships—whether chronically conflictual or chronically nonconflictual—must be dealt with to pave the way for authentic intimacy.

One of the surest avenues for strengthening self-differentiation is the assignment for each spouse to invest in building direct relationships with his or her extended family. The displacement and projection of unresolved issues from one relationship to another, or in some cases from one generation to another, is short-circuited when extended family relationships are strengthened, taking much of the strain off the marriage relationship.

Encouraging each of the partners to take a creatively different stance in the relationship is also an antidote to fusion. The playfulness of a new (less anxious and serious) perspective is often the catalyst for healthier personal boundaries and relational growth.

Conflict

Perhaps no area in marital interaction has received such astounding results, according to recent studies, as conflict. With the capacity to predict with a 94-percent accuracy whether marriages will succeed or fail, Gottman (1994) has underscored the importance of skill building and equipping for healthy conflict. Through the SYMBIS program, as well as marital counseling, we often teach couples the X, Y, Z formula—in situation X, when you do Y, I feel Z—to help them state their feelings (Markman, Stanley, and Blumberg 1994, 83–84). The use of this formula helps couples avoid the vicious cycle of criticism and contempt that Gottman has identified as fatal to marriage.

Another useful technique for dealing with marital conflict is the Conflict Card, which we have given to countless couples. We are not sure from where the idea came, but it has helped us resolve conflicts in our own marriage, and we have seen it work for hundreds of others. On the card is a scale from one to ten ranking the intensity of a person's feelings, ranging from one, "I'm not enthusiastic, but it's no big deal to me," to ten, "Over my dead body." Using an objective measurement of the intensity of feelings allows for a partner who tends to be less expressive to communicate on even ground with a more expressive partner.

Gender Differences

Research and experience consistently point to a fundamental and powerful distinction between the sexes. As we work with couples, we find that typically men try to meet needs that they value and women do the same. We believe that couples can celebrate male-female differences in marriage by accurately understanding and meeting the unique needs that are part of their spouse's gender. The recent work of Deborah Tannen (1990), *You Just Don't Understand*, is often prescribed by us and by others as bibliotherapy. In addition, based on the work of Howard Markman and S.A. Kraft (1989), we work with couples to highlight core needs of each gender. While there will always be exceptions to the rule, a wife's most basic needs in marriage are to be (a) cherished, (b) known, and (c) respected. Men, on the other hand, tend to desire (a) admiration, (b) autonomy, and (c) shared activity.

Marriage Myths

Plaguing every unsatisfied marriage is a vast assortment of myths about what marriage should be. Jeffrey Larson (1988) identified more than forty marital myths that cause problems. In our counseling and teaching, we address myths that spring from unspoken rules and unconscious roles in the family of origin. Helping the couples we counsel to become more aware of their unspoken rules can keep little problems from becoming big ones. We often have each of the partners complete an exercise entitled, "Your Personal Ten Commandments." This exercise is designed to identify the expectations that emerge (almost involuntarily) from their family backgrounds, sibling positions, and personal dispositions. Making secret (unconscious) expectations known allows for conscious examination and incorporation or elimination.

To generate material for the personal commandments, we often provide a list of incomplete sentence stems, such as the following, for each partner to complete.

> Women are . . . Men are . . . Sex is . . . Children are . . . Success is . . . Failure is . . . Being a woman and having a career is . . . Being a man and having a career is . . . Spirituality is . . . Being self-giving is . . .

The responses are then reworded as commands. Here is a sampling of the rules we have heard from couples:

> Men should not ask for help unless they are desperate.
>
> Women should always downplay their career successes.
>
> Men should never act too happy.
>
> Children should never get sick.
>
> Married people should not be too serious about anything.
>
> Spouses should not buy expensive gifts for each other—money should be spent on gifts for the kids.
>
> Husbands and wives should never kiss before noon.
>
> Women should never go to bed before cleaning the kitchen.
>
> Husbands and wives should never talk about sex with anyone but each other.

Breaking an unspoken rule can be perceived as a sign of betrayal to each partner. Never talking about unspoken rules is like walking through a marital minefield. Heightening awareness can help the couple avoid needless explosions. It will help them recognize their freedom to accept, reject, challenge, and change their rules for relating.

Guilt

In a survey assessing "who makes you feel most guilty," the majority of respondents confessed they were the key perpetrators of their own guilt. But next on the list was "my spouse." Thirty-seven percent of married people reported that their spouses control them through guilt. In our work with couples, we consider four marriage styles, which result from different mixtures of love and guilt in the same person: the pleaser, controller, withholder, and lover (Les Parrott 1994). We offer suggestions for personal change as well as healthy and loving responses to pleasing, controlling, and withholding marriage partners.

Task 1
Respond to the case study by telling precisely how you might typically treat it, in how many sessions, in what order, and with what responses by the clients throughout counseling. One restriction: Assume that between the third and fourth counseling sessions with you— regardless of what had gone on during the previous session—the couple had a major argument and come to the fourth session in some crisis.

As cotherapists, we would approach Art and Pam's situation from two angles: (a) family-systems perspective and (b) attention to special issues in the relationship. Because Art and Pam are highly motivated to work on their relationship issues, our therapeutic work with this couple would probably require between three and six months of weekly sessions.

Since we assume the initial intake interviews have occurred (information is provided by the case study), the first four to six weeks of therapy for Art and Pam would involve reducing their focus on the marriage and placing their relationship in the broader context of their extended families through (a) constructing a genogram, (b) assessing family-of-origin relationships, and (c) reestablishing connections with the family of origin. This therapeutic approach seems to have great merit for couples who have become myopic and see their partners as the source of all pain and joy in their lives. Art and Pam may have transferred their parental struggles (for Art distance, for Pam fusion) to each other directly. The presenting issue with the couple is intimacy.

Constructing Family Genograms

Pam and Art are trapped in a pattern of distancer-pursuer, which we would approach by constructing a genogram for Art and for Pam that incorporates information about family structure, functioning information, and critical life-cycle events. Patterns of emotional distance, cutoff, conflict, and relational triangles will be explored through family myths, rules, roles, relationships, legacies, and so on. Particular attention will be paid to the level of self-differentiation of each. Several indications in the case material suggest a fairly low level of differentiation: (a) Art's half-hearted "rebellious" (as defined by him) decision to become an engineer rather than a scientist; his own disengaged or "spiritless" family of origin; and his attachment to the aunt and uncle (who died when he was an adolescent), and (b) Pam's "conversion" from Catholicism to Protestant Christianity and her overly close family (cutting off and then reestablishing, becoming angry then reinitiating weekly lunches).

Assessing Family-of-Origin Dynamics

Given the presenting information about both partners' family systems, we would use the FACES III (Olson, Russell, and Sprenkle 1979, 1983) to measure perceived and ideal levels of cohesion and adaptability of the families of each. The Family Adaptability and Cohesion Scales (FACES III) is a 20-item instrument designed to measure two main dimensions of family functioning: cohesion (relational proximity) and adaptability (ability to change). The instrument places families within the Circumplex Model by assessing how family members see their family (perceived) and how they would like it to be (ideal). Results of this assessment identify 16 types of marital and family systems based on each family's degree of cohesion and adaptability. Each dimension has four levels (very low, low to moderate, moderate to high, and very high), which creates a 4 x 4 design.

A note about cultural difference. Art and Pam come from culturally different families. However, it is our belief that although culture plays an important role in family process, culture is "the medium through which family process works its art" (Friedman 1989, 122). Bearing this in mind, we would continue to be sensitive to cultural themes, but we would seek to do so in a way that does not allow culture to camouflage family process. In the case of Art and Pam, the most obvious link to the family process is the "spiritless" family of Art and the spirited, energetically invested style of Pam's Italian-American family. The underlying issue, again, seems to be intimacy and connection.

Reworking Family-of-Origin Relationships

From our perspective, the same emotional process that Art and Pam are experiencing in their relationship was operating in their families of origin. Only limited improvement of their relationship will occur without work by each of them in the family of origin. We would encourage each of them to spend individual time with, or make contact with, every family member. Their objective is not to confront or accuse, but rather to become aware of the tone and type of intimacy they experience with each one.

Art may be able to draw on his "scientific" skills to reconnect with his family, while observing how they interact. If possible, we would encourage Art to discuss his infertility and affair with his father and mother separately. We would encourage Pam to discuss her firing at work as well as her career dreams with her father and mother separately. (For the time being, it would be off-limits for Pam to discuss Art's affair or for Art to discuss Pam's firing.) A strategic plan to foster increased self-differentiation (the ability to stay present and nonanxious) within their families will be implemented over time.

It is to be expected that after a measure of rewarding work by Art and by Pam within the family of origin, an intense conflict will erupt between the couple. At this point, it is important to begin to address specific current issues between the couple.

Addressing the Hurt of Being Fired

Being fired can have a significant impact on the family system (Parrott and Parrott 1995a). Counselors have noticed surprising similarities in the struggles suffered by families of the terminally ill and families of a terminated employee (Moracco, Butche, and Collins 1991). Each terminated individual experiences poor self-esteem and negative emotions leading to depression. The most common and debilitating psychological effect of job loss is self-blame. Research shows that not dealing with the hurt and anger of job loss can result in self-sabotage in the job-search process (Willensky 1993).

We would ask Pam to purchase a journal and write about her job-loss experience. Her assignment would be to find a quiet place and write, without censoring content or attending to spelling or grammar, for about twenty minutes on at least five consecutive days. This intervention will help Pam to open up, get her feelings on paper, and bring closure to the trauma of being fired. A dialogue between Art and Pam regarding her reflections will be facilitated.

Addressing the Hurt of Infertility

As a couple, Art and Pam are facing the major hurt of infertility with all of its resultant grief, blame, and disequilibrium. Because infertility is a disruption in the natural life-cycle flow for Art and Pam, the increased pain it introduces into their marital system may have caused a quantum leap in anxiety, intensifying their entrenched style of relating.

Infertility can have devastating impact on a marriage relationship. Art and Pam are experiencing the crisis of infertility, and they must work at redefining the purpose of their shared future. Every area of

125

the couple's life has been affected, from career decisions (particularly for Pam) to sexual function to relationships with extended family members. The impact on relationships with extended family is seen clearly in their sudden decision to move back home.

For a woman, bearing a child is often considered a confirmation of her femininity and a rite of passage into legitimate adulthood. This may be particularly true in Pam's case since the role of a woman in her mind may be closely associated with her mother who did not work outside of the home but "reared six children as 'good Roman Catholics.'" At thirty-eight, Pam may feel that fulfillment in her life is severely threatened. Art, who is already uncomfortable with intimacy, may feel threatened and frustrated as he listens to the freely shared grief of his wife. Because the infertility problem was identified as his, he may suffer doubts about his masculinity, as well. (These doubts may be crucially relevant to his affair, which resulted in decreased sexual satisfaction between Art and Pam, since she was now feeling "irritated" by his sexual stimulation.) In addition to addressing this experience as a backdrop for their ongoing struggle for intimacy, we would work at affirming them as a couple and as gifted and whole persons, even if they are unable to have children. Our goal would be to help Art and Pam focus on their strengths and value their contributions. This may be particularly important for Pam since the failure to bear children follows closely after a professional failure.

We would address the phases that couples facing infertility typically go through as an avenue for exploring the unique experience of Art and Pam (Leslie Parrott 1994). First, couples tend to question why this is happening to them. What have they done wrong? Why are they so defective? Why are they denied something the rest of the world takes for granted? Next, couples mourn the loss of ability to bear children. They search their souls for many months to determine what, exactly, this will mean for them and their future identity within the extended family and society. Finally, the couple enters a decision-making phase. They will either pursue adoption or begin to seek fulfillment in other ways. It is helpful to underscore that the shock, anger, and self-blame that lead to acceptance may take more than a year to come to completion.

Addressing the Affair

We would address Art's brief adulterous affair and the resultant impact it has had on their intimacy, passion, and commitment. This situation calls us to create space for confession and forgiveness as well as keen understanding from the systemic dynamics. Art's affair may be interpreted in several ways: as an attempt to prove his manhood after being diagnosed as sterile; as an attempt to rebel and individuate from his family of origin and, by extension, from Pam; and as an attempt to maintain a triangle to regulate the level of intimacy in the marriage relationship since Pam is no longer distracted by her work, which may have acted as a sort of "mistress" for the marriage, nor does she have a baby to focus on. Spiritual-guidance techniques may be sensitively applied to bring about forgiveness and reaffirmation of mutual commitment.

Designing Forgiveness and Commitment Rituals

Rituals have been described as the most elegant synthesis of intervention and technique (Watzlawick 1978). Forgiveness and reaffirmation of a covenantal commitment to the marriage deserve a ritual that will serve as a symbolic marker for the couple. We would prescribe a therapeutic ritual to embody forgiveness and another to embody a renewal in marital commitment. These rituals would be designed by the couple and would engage each partner in meaningful shared activity, perhaps with the culmination of an exchange of vows or a shared communion.

Task 2
Create a dialogue between the counselor and the couple (or one spouse, if you prefer) showing how you might deal with communication difficulties.

Art and Pam came to their counseling session anxious and depressed. Both of them felt that their marriage was sinking because of increasing conflict. In their last fight, after a loud and ugly shouting match, Pam called Art "an egotistical, self-satisfied, nonexpressive lump who is more interested in himself and his needs than in meeting any of my [her] needs." Over time, Art and Pam have experienced a continued inability to communicate. As cotherapists, we attempt to move the focus from the content of the issues to the process of their interaction and the underlying intimacy issues.

Pam: Things are terrible. Art won't stop picking on me. "Find a job, keep the kitchen clean, don't take yourself so seriously, don't call your mom so often."

Les: What would you say to that, Art?

Art: If she's so eager to be in charge of something, I think she should get a job, not control me. It's not like she has to become some corporate mogul or happy housekeeper. It's for her benefit as much as mine. She's happiest when she feels like her life is under control.

Pam: He just doesn't realize that it takes time. I'll get back on track, but it takes some time, that's all.

Leslie: Art, Pam says you're rushing her. How much time will you give her? Is there a date circled on the calendar?

Art: No, it's not like that. But she's been saying that for months. I mean, some of this was going on before the whole thing with her boss and before we got the test results—no kids.

Les: Art, would you consider yourself a success in getting Pam to change?

Art: Sometimes, if I am upset enough. She usually cries, says I'm right, and does change. In January, she got very into her job search. She had an index-card file with contacts and was setting up at least one appointment a week. She seemed enthusiastic and into it for a while, but she only kept it up for a couple of weeks.

Leslie: Maybe you're not trying hard enough.

128

Art: That's a good one! I go through this every day as it is.

Les: Maybe if you reminded her more often.

Art: No way. It's hard enough as it is. I'm just trying to get enough peace and quiet to keep myself going.

Leslie: You could try thinking more about her problems. Maybe if you approached them more logically or rationally.

Art: More? I've analyzed them too much already. I guess it's not too effective.

Les: How would you explain your lack of effectiveness in trying to fix Pam?

Pam: Fix me! He just wants to make me different, to be just like him.

Leslie: Art, Pam makes it sound like you're choreographing her character in a movie.

Art: That's a new one, but she's definitely the director. Anyway, why shouldn't she want to be more productive and happy? I wish she would.

Les: Well, everyone knows when a woman doesn't take care of her home, she really doesn't love her husband.

Leslie: Besides, if she got a job, people wouldn't notice how depressed she is about not having a baby.

Art: Sometimes I think that.

Les: Pam, when did you stop loving Art? When did you start thinking life with him wasn't enough to make you happy?

Pam: I love him, and I want a life with him, but I feel so powerless to please him. No matter what I do, I just can't.

Leslie: Art, can you make Pam hurt and defensive whenever you want to?

Art: Without fail. I've got that one down to a science!

Les: If you were going to draw me a foolproof blueprint to get Pam to justify herself, how would it look?

Art:	It's not like I do it on purpose.
Les:	I'm not saying you do, but just suppose, what would you do?
Art:	Tell her she could find a job if she really wanted one.
Pam:	You're right. I know I could. The recession is over and I'm getting connections through church. But I think I do a pretty good job with the kitchen, with the whole house really.
Art:	You used to, before we got the test results.
Leslie:	Art, what made you say that then?
Art:	When she looks at me that way, it makes me really mad.
Leslie:	Looks what way?
Art:	I don't know; it's the eyes.
Les:	What about the eyes? Does she roll them? Look right at you? Look away? What?
Art:	I told you, I don't know. I guess it's all of those.
Leslie:	Wait a minute, do you mean that all Pam has to do is give you that look and you jump? Pam, if you've gotten that look down pat, you can get Art uptight every time you want.
Art:	She tries, but I don't think she has that much control over me.
Les:	Maybe, but it doesn't sound like you have a free spirit.
Art:	Well, maybe I am overly sensitive.
Leslie:	Pam, what is your response to that?
Pam:	If he's so sensitive, why doesn't he know how much he hurts me?
Les:	Art?
Art:	I've heard a lot from her too, especially how her whole life is empty since she can't have a baby. I can't do anything about it. And it's not my fault she lost her job.
Pam:	Well, grief isn't something I can control, you know. I need to be able to cry on your shoulder. That's what a husband does when he loves his wife.
Leslie:	Wow. I wonder if you two should strike a deal? Art

will let you cry on his shoulder whenever you need to, and you can go out and find a job.

Pam: That's stupid. They're not the same thing at all. He wants me to get a job to show I'm all better; I need to cry so I can get better. I just want to be loved—but what he wants is for me to change.

Les: Art, what would you say to that?

Art: All I want is what is good for her.

Leslie: Pam, when Art pushes you harder to get a job or clean the house, how does that impact you?

Pam: It saps my energy instantly. I mean, I'm always wanting these things myself, but when he gets sarcastic, I run the opposite direction just to be safe.

Leslie: Pam, why does your husband have so much power to determine your goals for you?

Pam: That's a good question. I just love him too much and want his approval.

Les: It seems to me that if you two keep loving each other so much, you might destroy each other. How would you both see the difference between pleasing, controlling, and loving?

Pam: I guess I always thought they were a lot alike. That's why I try to tell Art clearly what my needs are—so he can meet them.

Art: I don't think they're the same at all. When Pam needs me to please her or tries to control me, I don't feel loved. But, I have to admit, I didn't realize how much I bank my emotions on whether or not Pam is happy and seems to be active and productive. I may be more of a pleaser than I want to be.

Leslie: Pam, how do you deal with the double message, be close and loving, but not needy?

Pam: I always knew Art didn't want me to be needy, so I didn't think he loved me. What I never realized before is that Art is needy sometimes—that's why he's always on my case.

131

References

Bowen, M. 1978. *Family therapy in clinical practice.* New York: Jason Aronson.

Carter, B., and M. McGoldrick. 1989. *The changing family life cycle: A framework for family therapy.* 2d ed. Boston: Allyn and Bacon.

Friedman, E. H. 1985. *Generation to generation: Family process in church and synagogue.* New York: Guilford.

————. 1989. Systems and ceremonies: A family view of rites of passage. In *The changing family life cycle: A framework for family therapy,* edited by B. Carter and M. McGoldrick, 2d ed. Boston: Allyn and Bacon.

Gilbert, R. M. 1992. *Extraordinary relationships: A new way of thinking about human interactions.* Minneapolis: CHRONIMED Publishing.

Gottman, J. M. 1994. *Why marriages succeed or fail.* New York: Simon and Schuster.

Kerr, M. 1992. Forward to *Extraordinary relationships: A new way of thinking about human interactions,* by R. M. Gilbert, pp. vii–xi. Minneapolis: CHRONIMED Publishing.

Koman, S. L., and G. Stechler. 1985. Making the jump to systems. In *Handbook of adolescents and family therapy,* edited by M. P. Mirkin and S. L. Komen, 3–19. New York: Gardner Press.

Larson, J. H. 1988. The marriage quiz: College students' beliefs in selected myths about marriage. *Family Relations* 37:3–11.

Lasswell, M. 1985. Illusions regarding marital happiness. *Medial Aspects of Human Sexuality* 19:144–58.

Markman, H. J., and S. A. Kraft. 1989. Men and women in marriage: Dealing with gender differences in marital therapy. *Behavior Therapist* 12:51–56.

Markman, H. J., S. M. Stanley, and S. L. Blumberg. 1994. *Fighting for your marriage.* San Francisco: Jossey-Bass.

Markman, H. J., S. M. Stanley, F. J. Floyd, and S. L. Blumberg. 1991. The Premarital Relationship Enhancement Program (PREP): Current status. *Family Relations.*

Moracco, J., P. Butche, and M. Collins. 1991. Professional career services: An explanatory study. *Journal of Employment Counseling* 28:21–28.

Olson, D., D. G. Fourier, and J. M. Druckman. 1987. *Counselor's manual for PREPARE/ENRICH.* rev. ed. Minneapolis: PREPARE/ENRICH, Inc.

Olson, D., C. Russell, and D. Sprenkle. 1979. Circumplex model of marital and family systems: I. Cohesion and adaptability dimensions, family types, and clinical applications. Theoretical update. *Family Process* 18:3–28.

———. 1983. Circumplex model of marital and family systems: IV. Theoretical update. *Family Process* 22:69–83.

Rilke, R. M. 1954. *Letters to a young poet.* Translated by M. D. Hester. New York: Norton.

Parrott, Les, III. 1994. *Love's unseen enemy: How to overcome guilt to build healthy relationships.* Grand Rapids: Zondervan.

Parrott, Les, III, and Leslie Parrott. 1995b. *Saving your marriage before it starts: Seven questions to ask before (and after) you marry.* New York: HaperCollins.

Parrott, Leslie. 1994. Infertility and pregnancy counseling. In *Leadership handbooks of practical theology: Outreach and care,* edited by J. D. Berkely, 2:322–23. Grand Rapids: Baker.

Parrott, Leslie, and Les Parrott III. 1995a. *The career counselor: Guidance for planning careers and managing career crises.* Dallas: Word Books.

Tannen, D. 1990. *You just don't understand: Women and men in conversation.* New York: Ballatine.

Toman, W. 1976. *Family constellation,* 3d ed. New York: Springer.

Warren, N. C. 1992. *Finding the love of your life.* Colorado Springs: Focus on the Family.

Waltzlawick, P. 1978. *The language of change.* New York: Basic Books.

Willensky, D. 1993. Writing off the unemployment blues. *American Health* 12:35.

Worthington, E. L., Jr. 1989. *Marriage counseling: A Christian approach to counseling couples.* Downers Grove, Ill.: InterVarsity.

Christian PREP

An Empirically Based Model for Marital and Premarital Intervention

Scott M. Stanley, Daniel W. Trathen, and Savanna C. McCain

Christian PREP (Prevention and Relationship Enhancement Program) is a cognitive-behavioral model for intervention with premarital or marital couples in either counseling or program settings (Stanley, Trathen, and McCain 1992). PREP embodies an approach for working with couples based on years of empirical research at the University of Denver and elsewhere (Markman, Floyd, Stanley, and Lewis 1986). Though originally designed for preventing marital distress, the strategies of PREP are equally well suited for intervention with distressed couples. "Christian" PREP is founded on Scripture, with the integration of proven, empirically based strategies from PREP.

Question 1
What are the basics of your theory of marriage counseling? In your description, include your view of the typical cause(s) of marital problems and the typical goals of counseling.

Our approach is based on the belief that God has provided guidelines for marriage in Scripture. Furthermore, God allows us to learn more about the workings of relationships through sound research. The belief guiding our integration of Scripture and research is that all truth is God's truth, with Scripture being preeminent.

Consistent with Genesis 2, the key biblical theme of marriage is reflected in the teaching of Jesus that "they are no longer two, but one" (Matt. 19:6 NIV; Eph. 5). Yet, the union of husband and wife is beset with barriers to intimacy and oneness as a consequence of the fall. Both Scripture and research findings explicitly describe processes that destroy relationships.

The Mystery of Oneness

While Scripture teaches principles for healthy and growing marriages (e.g., Song of Songs; 1 Cor. 13; Eph. 5), oneness is described as a mystery by Paul (Eph. 5:32). Even though Paul is calling attention to the relationship of Christ and his church, it seems that the more general point holds as well—that oneness in marriage is a mysterious phenomenon. "Mystery" implies that God brings about a unique blending of the two spouses without specifying an exact pattern for oneness that must be emulated. In contrast, research demonstrates that distressed couples tend to be quite similar in their distress, displaying very predictable patterns of negative interaction and thinking. Where Scripture and research strikingly overlap is in the description of these negative patterns that destroy relationships and oneness.

Destructive Interaction

While there are many factors that raise the risk of distress and divorce, the most powerful predictors concern the destructive ways in which couples handle conflict and disagreement (Markman and Hahlweg 1993). Research from major marital research labs (e.g., ours—headed by our colleague Howard Markman—and John Gottman's at the University of Washington) suggests that the manner in which couples handle conflict predicts future breakup or divorce with over 90-percent accuracy (key patterns are highlighted in Markman, Stanley, and Blumberg 1994). For example, patterns such as escalation (returning negative for negative), invalidation (subtle or direct put-downs), and withdrawal (turning away, shutting down, or leaving the conversation) are excellent predictors of marital breakdown, and more so than positive dimensions like validation.

The case for the destructiveness of these kinds of patterns is clearly made in Scripture (e.g., Prov. 12:18; 15:1; 29:11; Eph. 4:25–27). In fact, 1 Peter 3:9–10 nicely summarizes the best research regarding marital success: "Do not repay evil with evil or insult with insult, but with blessing, because to this you were called so that you may inherit a blessing. For, 'Whoever would love life and see good days/must keep his tongue from evil and his lips from deceitful speech'" (NIV). The driving force behind destructive interaction is selfishness and self-protection—in other words, a failure to love one another (Gal. 5:13–15). This view of marital distress has major implications for helping couples. It is critical that preventive or interventive efforts be aimed at helping couples control negativity. Boosting positives is important, but it pales in comparison to the need for couples to learn how to manage conflict effectively (Stanley, Markmam, St. Peters, and Leber 1995). When the negative side of the relationship is handled skillfully, the foundation is set for oneness to occur according to the unique blending by God of the two.

Foundational Assumptions of Christian PREP

Hence, our model proceeds from the following assumptions: First, marriage is designed by God to be a relationship characterized by growth, nurturance, and the mystery of oneness expressing itself in love. Second, because of sin and the fall, marriages are plagued by the erection of barriers to oneness, most notably those formed out of self-protective motives. Third, the accompanying conflict— which in certain forms is very predictive of marital breakdown and divorce—precludes oneness from occurring because it is not safe for vulnerability to occur in the relationship.

In this regard, Adam's reply, when he was hiding in the garden, to God is enlightening: "I was afraid because I was naked; so I hid" (Gen. 3:10 NIV). In marriage, people hide themselves out of fear of rejection. Note that Adam and Eve first covered the features that were most different between them. What *could be* and what *was meant to be* the very basis of great intimacy and union became something to hide out of fear. Whether seen as a cause or result of such fear (or both), couples regularly resort to various negative and destructive patterns in their handling of differences which preclude oneness from developing. When marriage becomes safer—because of right motivations, behavior, and thinking—the blessings of intimacy can and usually do happen. Most people truly want intimacy to occur, but in not knowing how to deal with conflict constructively, there is no way they can experience it because intimacy requires a degree of security and safety that is so difficult for them to attain.

Hence, many of the most specific interventions in the Christian PREP model are aimed at helping couples structure negativity—by placing boundaries on when and how they will deal with the most dangerous issues in marriage. People do not generally learn such skills growing up, but they readily grasp the importance of them when presented with this approach. Even when couples are more distressed and less motivated, one of the most powerful things they can experience is that things can change. As they see changes occur, hope can begin to grow, which supplies more motivation for even greater change.

The PREP approach is quite different from general models of communication that teach sound skills but do not emphasize enough—in our view—how and when to implement them. We believe that couples benefit most by learning strategies for interrupting negative cycles *as they are happening*. Better still, they can learn how to protect their oneness from destructive conflict in the first place. There are no theoretical or empirical reasons in this model to assume that the best ways to prevent distress are much different from the best interventions to ameliorate distress after the fact. It is just that the latter is much harder to do.

How Marriages Die

We end our response to Question 1 with an explanation of how a marriage dies as understood within the context of the PREP model. Most couples start out with a great deal of positive energy, experience, and motivation. While the oneness achieved early in a marriage may not be the depth that is possible years later, there is a joy and delight in all of what oneness means to the couple, including intimacy in spiritual, emotional, intellectual, and physical forms. (We acknowledge that spiritual intimacy may be much more elusive for many couples, and Christian PREP does encourage couples to grow in such intimacy.)

As time goes on, the couple is confronted with the decisions of life: where to live, what career or job to have, whether or when to have children, how to deal with finances, and so on. The sheer number and complexity of decisions offer the couple many more opportunities for conflict than they experienced while dating. Whatever their conflict-management skills coming into marriage, these skills will be taxed to greater and greater degrees. Since most couples never learn to handle conflict, damaging interactions become more and more frequent.

Several problems predominate. First, couples do not set times and conditions—Ground Rules in our model—that place boundaries around conflict and its effects. Second, when in conflict, many couples do not have the skills to deal with it effectively, giving way to unproductive conflict and barriers. Third, to make matters worse, the mounting frustration leads to waning commitment levels and heightened selfishness. This raises anxiety and tension in the marriage because the most basic questions are triggered—for example, "Are you going to stay with me?" It becomes less and less safe to be vulnerable as the barriers solidify.

As an example of this process, consider the typical couple who has gone out to have a nice evening together. In the absence of any particular rule or skill for tabling conflicts that arise, conflicts can disrupt the evening. Worse, since the couple is poor at dealing with conflict, the evening is likely to be ruined if conflict does come up. The effect of numerous such experiences is that the two begin to feel as if they are walking in a mine field. There is little predictability about when the next unpleasant event will occur, but the abiding sense is that it will occur. The general effect on the marriage is devastating. Each partner begins to associate the presence of the other with the potential for painful conflict, not life-giving oneness. Often, a particularly destructive form of conflict management ensues, with one partner pursuing their dealing with issues (usually the female) and one partner withdrawing from the pursuit (usually the male). As one husband put it, "The reason I avoid talking with my wife is that I've noticed that talking leads to fighting."

In summary, the preeminent goals of Christian PREP are to interfere directly with the development and maintenance of unproductive and self-focused styles of relating. This is accomplished by teaching skills, techniques, and structures for constructively handling difficult issues, along with models for enhancing commitment and ensuring that forgiveness happen. In this context, the blessings of oneness can come to fruition.

Question 2
For what kind of people is your approach most appropriate?

Our approach is appropriate for premarital and marital couples, whether distressed or not. It can be implemented effectively by pastors and mental-health professionals (Stanley, Markham, St. Peters, and Leber 1995). While the interventions apply equally well to various kinds of couples, the method of delivery can be varied, depending on the needs of couples.

For example, PREP was originally developed out of a long tradition of studies aimed at the prevention of distress and divorce (Markman et al. 1986) and thus has most often been delivered as a five- or six-session premarital program. As such, PREP has been tested in a major longitudinal study of marriage at the University of Denver. The study was supported by grants from the National Institute of Mental Health and the National Science Foundation. Couples participating in PREP, as compared to matched controls, have been shown to have lower rates of breakup, lower frequencies of negative interactional styles, greater satisfaction, and lower incidence of physical aggression for years after delivery of the program (Markman et al. 1993). These findings suggest that prevention is a reasonable goal, but only if the targets are wisely chosen. Ongoing studies are comparing various other groups, such as a study by Daniel Trathen (1995) contrasting Christian PREP with a typical information-based program for premarital couples within evangelical churches.

The goals and techniques of PREP are just as applicable for distressed couples as they are for premarital couples or for early marital couples who are not distressed. This is logically so since the same kinds of patterns that reliably predict future problems also discriminate currently distressed couples from those who are not. With seriously distressed couples, the delivery of the model in a counseling setting is likely to be more effective than in a program/group setting.

Christian PREP has been well received in a wide variety of Christian groups. That positive reaction is by design—Christian PREP presents foundational Christian truths about marriage without opening up discussions of more controversial doctrines. Groups using the model have latitude to supplement the material with other doctrinal emphases particular to the group or denomination.

Question 3
What are your foci for counseling?

The PREP model comes from a clear cognitive-behavioral tradition. Interventions are generally targeted at styles of thinking and behaving that reliably lead to emotional pain, turmoil, and distance. Since poorly handled conflict will erode a couple's attempts at oneness, many behavioral and cognitive interventions are employed to help couples short-circuit such processes.

Most of the behavioral interventions are specifically targeted at teaching couples how to communicate well and control conflict—and possibly grow closer during such times. This leads us to an important theorem of Christian PREP and cognitive-behavioral models in general: Just as insight (especially the kind that leads to repentance) can produce changes in behavior, changes in behavior can lead to powerful changes in insight. When Christ says to "first clean the inside of the cup and dish, then the outside also will be clean" (Matt. 23:26 NIV), his reference is clearly to the need for change to occur on the inside that works its way out. But his point is less directly about insight than right motivation (e.g., as derived from repentance).

Without discounting that life-change can follow insight, we have seen many couples who have excellent insights—for example, about family of origin—without demonstrable changes occurring in the way they live. Consider a situation wherein a wife has formed, with some justification, a strong belief that her husband does not care about her compared to other interests in his life. They could explore family-of-origin experiences that predisposed him to certain patterns of marital neglect. Perhaps, as research shows is often the case, he has learned to avoid his wife because he is not comfortable with his ability to handle marital conflict. He believes that his wife wants to start fights by continually bringing up disagreements. All the insight in the world does not meet the legitimate desire of this wife to be more connected with her husband and the legitimate desire of this husband to have less conflict with his wife.

In PREP, the wife and husband would be taught when and where not to deal with conflictual issues and how to communicate and solve problems with more respect and safety. If the partners each learn that they can effectively communicate, even when in conflict, this behavior change will produce a powerful change in insight. In learning, practicing, and mastering a new way of relating, the wife receives a great deal of evidence contrary to the belief she has formed that he does not care. He receives a great deal of evidence contrary to the belief he has formed that she desires to nag and raise conflict as a matter of course. These are powerful changes in cognitive insight due to the observance of behavioral change (i.e., experience).

Question 4
How is your marriage counseling conducted?

As in a systematic desensitization model, couples can learn to overcome their anxiety about conflict and intimacy by learning new attitudes and behavior in a way that gradually draws them closer without destructive processes occurring—at least as frequently. The resulting effect on the emotional climate of the marriage can be significant.

Key cognitive interventions are also employed with the goal of causing changes in understanding about the self and relationship. For example, empirical research clearly points out that distressed couples tend to adopt very negative attribution patterns, with negative events attributed to the partner's character and positive events attributed to chance (Baucom and Epstein 1990). We present a communication model to help couples understand how beliefs, emotions, and differences in style can cause filtering of real meanings and lead to misinterpretations. In this context, we point out the dangers of seeking evidence to fit what one already believes—especially when beliefs are rigidly negative about the partner.

Other cognitive interventions take place in the context of commitment theory (Stanley and Markman 1991, 1992). The theory presented helps couples distinguish two key forms of commitment, constraint and dedication, and further helps couples to maintain an emphasis on dedication as a reservoir of motivation for positive investment in the marriage. The empirical literature on dedication nicely overlays the biblical concept of *agape* love, which adds to the meaning of passages such as 1 Corinthians 13 from both biblical and empirical perspectives.

Also in the cognitive realm, couples are encouraged to consider the types, reasonableness, and explicitness of many of the expectations they hold in the relationship. Couples are taught how certain kinds of expectations are clearly linked with greater conflict and the destruction of oneness rather than the promotion of a shared worldview as a couple.

Question 5
How do you deal with a few of the common marital problems?

The PREP approach employs a variety of behavioral (skills) and cognitive interventions in order to help couples learn how to nourish oneness in all its forms. To help couples create the climate for oneness, many interventions are aimed at better conflict management. We will describe just two of them (for more details, see Stanley, Markman, and Blumberg 1992, 1994).

The premise is that couples can handle conflict, differences, and disagreements more effectively to the extent that they have agreed upon structures or maps for doing so. For example, one of the numerous Ground Rules we teach couples is that "Either one can bring up an issue at any time, but the listener has the right to say, 'This is not a good time.' If the listener says 'this is not a good time,' he or she takes the responsibility to find a good time within the next twenty-four hours." This may sound like an extremely simple Ground Rule, and, in fact, it is. Simplicity can be powerful. Based on biblical principles, research, and experience with couples, we are amazed at how few couples are aware of very basic rules for structuring conflict. Most couples live as if it were always open season for conflict, thereby living with the corrosive effects on their ability to maintain oneness. While some couples may refuse to put down the battle gear, most couples seem able to benefit greatly from such Ground Rules.

As the stated Ground Rule implies, couples need to deal constructively with issues that will come up in life. The problem is that most couples communicate the worst when they need to do it the best—during conflict. What could be opportunities for deepening the relationship become experiences of frustration and deepening alienation. We teach couples the Speaker/Listener Technique as a method for communicating effectively when it counts most (Stanley, Markman, and Blumberg 1991, 1994; Markman, Stanley, and Blumberg 1992, 1994). This technique is very specific, very simple in structure, and, therefore, very effective when a couple really needs the help. Couples use "the floor" to designate the speaker, and rules for the speaker and listener roles are defined. We provide couples with the floor, which is a small piece of card-stock on which the rules for the technique are printed. The speaker speaks for himself or herself and keeps statements relatively brief. The listener edits out his or her tendency to rebut and focuses on the speaker's message, showing listening by paraphrasing. The partners take turns in the roles by passing the floor when desired.

When couples use the technique, the emphasis is on discussing problems with respect and validation for one another's opinion, even when there is disagreement. We tell couples that it is a very specific way to put James 1:19 into effect: "My dear brothers, take note of this: Everyone should be quick to listen, slow to speak and slow to become angry" (NIV). The key is for couples to practice the technique and learn to engage it when they need to. The rules bring to conversations much needed structure, which by theory and research is believed to make it much harder for escalation, invalidation, and withdrawal to occur.

We have focused our interventions on simple rather than complex models because we believe complex models are not likely to be very helpful to couples. Couples can neither easily remember nor employ them when in conflict. It is also our experience that when a few basic rules are followed, most of the other desirable communication behaviors begin to happen without being specified. When partners can communicate well on difficult topics, they are practicing the biblical ideal of oneness that allows both for individuality and an abiding sense of the whole—working as a team.

The value of structure when things get tough is emphasized in many ways. For example, Christian PREP teaches a step-by-step model, which is based on Jesus' teaching, for working through forgiveness (e.g., Mark 11:25; Matt. 18). We emphasize steps, not as a substitute for a heart willing to forgive, but as a path for two to walk when their hearts are ready to forgive as Christ commands.

To demonstrate our approach, we will describe one cognitive intervention consistent with the PREP model and the integration of Scripture and research. Commitment theory and research suggest that people who are more dedicated to their mates spend less time considering the alternatives to the marriage, most specifically, other people (Stanley and Markman 1992). They also tend to devalue mentally the attractiveness of those alternatives that do exist in order to preserve their commitment to the marriage (Johnson and Rusbult 1989). These findings suggest powerful cognitive strategies for the protection of commitment in marriage, and they cast a fascinating light on Malachi 2:16 where God says, "I hate divorce." This passage is preceded by the command to "guard yourself in your spirit, and do not break faith with the wife of your youth" (v. 15 NIV). What more effective way to guard oneself in one's spirit than by cognitively reducing the tendency to think about being with others and, when tempted, by looking for why the grass is *not* greener?

There are many more interventions, both cognitive and behavioral, in the Christian PREP model. Those described here will serve to give the reader a basic understanding of the theory and type of techniques flowing from the integration of Scripture and sound research. We believe couples seeking services are generally looking for specific, practical suggestions that make a difference. To this end, Christian PREP helps couples deal with their issues through an integrated model of marriage as God designed it.

Task 1
Respond to the case study by telling precisely how you might typically treat it, in how many sessions, in what order, and with what responses by the clients throughout counseling. One restriction: Assume that between the third and fourth counseling sessions with you—regardless of what had gone on during the previous session—the couple had a major argument and come to the fourth session in some crisis.

Art and Pam's oneness and intimacy have been seriously eroded by their inability to handle the problems they have faced. Their bickering and fighting have pushed the relationship to a place of chronic negativity. These negative interactions along with the affair have done great damage to trust, resulting in an intense fear of vulnerability that now pervades their marriage. The good news is that there is some commitment, providing a starting point for rebuilding a lost love.

Session 1

The therapist first gathered a solid but brief understanding of Art and Pam's problems and goals. It became clear that they needed a great deal of help with communication and conflict management. Their despair made it crucial that they be given a framework of hope and be introduced to the Christian PREP model of therapy. In Revelation 2:4–5 Christ admonishes the Ephesians because they have left their "first love." The instructions for regaining first love are as relevant in marriage as they are in our devotion to the Lord: (a) remember, (b) repent, and (c) "do the works you did at first" (v. 5 NIV).

Hence, the therapist first asked Pam and Art to reminisce (i.e., remember) about better times, which stimulated their appetite for real change. Pam and Art brightened noticeably, which pointed to a

147

reservoir of positive affect that had not been entirely extinguished by years of bickering and defensiveness. The second step in Christ's model (i.e., repent) points to the importance of setting their minds toward real change. When asked if they really wanted to try to turn things around, each clearly expressed yes, allowing both to hear from the other a commitment to work hard. The last step Christ mentions leads directly to a description of the methods of Christian PREP. When Christ says, "[D]o the works you did at first," we see the clear need to do the kind of things done when love was stronger. Early on, partners are more polite, show more respect, make time, talk more like friends, listen better, show more zeal, and give greater evidence of passion in the bond of love. These "works" of love are the very things that Christian PREP teaches couples to preserve or regain. Jesus Christ's model points to a way and a hope.

The therapist explained up front to Art and Pam the rationale for working on their communication and conflict-management skills and described patterns that predict divorce, noting how the two of them exhibited classic patterns (e.g., the pursuer/withdrawer cycles). They were told how such patterns actively erode the positives over time. The therapist also briefly explained research suggesting that males usually distance themselves because of problems dealing with conflict in marriage, not because they do not care about intimacy (Markman, Stanley, and Blumberg 1994). Females, on the other hand, are more likely to seek closeness by talking, including discussing relationship problems. In contrast to Pam's belief that Art's distancing meant he just did not care and Art's belief that Pam just wanted to stir up conflict, both were soothed as they considered less negative interpretations for the frustrating behaviors. Explaining these negative patterns helped Pam and Art feel that they found a counselor with a clear understanding of their most pressing concerns and their difficulties were common marital issues.

At the end of the first session, the therapist gave Art and Pam homework in the *Fighting for Your Marriage* videos and in the Christian PREP Couple's Manual, all of which helped lay the foundation for the skills they would learn. The therapist also related the importance of their doing what is assigned. Pam and Art agreed to not attempt to talk about really difficult issues, except in therapy, for now. They were also given simple assessment forms to measure levels of satisfaction, commitment, and problem intensity.

At this point, the therapist's understanding of Art and Pam's relationship history was limited yet sufficient to know that their most pressing need was for better conflict management. More history was gathered as the skill base was built, and therapy moved into topics such as expectations and hidden issues.

Session 2

Pam and Art returned assessment forms, then moved directly to sharing their reactions to the other homework. They reported experiencing all the "danger signs," yet were encouraged because they could see reason for hope. The therapist then emphasized the systemic nature of their pursuer/withdrawer dynamics so that both were pressed to see how their style of conflict makes the other's more likely to continue—balancing responsibility between them for destructive conflict.

The therapist moved right to work on two hallmarks of the PREP approach: (a) the use of the Time-Out Ground Rule during sequences of escalating conflict and (b) the use of the Speaker/Listener Technique. Also introducing Art and Pam to the concept of filters, the therapist showed how they were each distorting and negatively interpreting many marital events. This discussion helped the two understand the ways in which their emotional styles (from their family backgrounds) led to many misinterpretations, even in routine conversations. In learning the Speaker/Listener Technique and agreeing to some common Ground Rules, Pam and Art began to recognize the value of structuring their interactions so that conflicts would be less damaging. By the end of this session, they had practiced the Speaker/Listener Technique with the coaching of the therapist. The active teaching also helped them understand that it was going to be relatively safe, at least in the therapist's office.

While Pam and Art were mostly very positive, Pam did express reservations that deeper issues were not being addressed. The therapist reassured her that deeper issues would be addressed, but that it would be wiser to do so when they learned to better handle painful issues. They were given homework that included instructions to practice the Speaker/Listener Technique several times before the next session using low-conflict issues. The therapist stressed that this is a time for learning new skills, not for resolving everything left unresolved over the previous sixteen years.

Session 3

Pam and Art reported some measured success with the homework. Several opportunities to use the Time-Out Ground Rule had occurred, with two successes and one failure. Art had attempted one Time Out without using the term, and Pam interpreted his withdrawal as unilateral and "the same old thing." Instructions for using Time Out were clarified.

Art and Pam's practicing of the Speaker/Listener Technique also went fairly well, but one practice session ended with a Time Out as things got too heated. The therapist praised them for having worked on these things over the week. They practiced more in this session, with the therapist actively coaching.

Session 4

Art and Pam came in to this session depressed and bitter. While practicing the Speaker/Listener Technique, they became embroiled in one of the greatest fights they have ever had. Art had thought they were progressing so well that he brought up his concerns about their sexual relationship and her being "colder than she used to be." This topic triggered major wounds from the past, both from the affair and from the infertility.

The therapist helped Pam and Art put their argument into some perspective. First, they were clearly not ready to discuss skillfully such a vulnerable topic. Second, paradoxically, Art had raised this sensitive issue because he felt they were making progress. This crisis opened up a deeper discussion of the dynamics of fear in their marriage and how each wanted to get closer but was terrified of rejection. As part of this discussion, the therapist taught from 1 John

4:18 about perfect love casting out fear. They could see how their fears would be more easily overcome if they could each meditate on the depth of God's love for them (especially as demonstrated by the cross, 1 John 4:10–18).

This crisis also afforded the opportunity to show Art and Pam the power of structure in helping to overcome fear and vulnerability. They were encouraged to try the conversation again, this time with the therapist coaching them firmly (see Task 2 on pp. 153–56). They engaged in one of the most healing and validating talks ever about their relationship. Each felt heard and gained confidence.

Session 5

In this session, Art and Pam reported tremendous progress. They had several successful experiences using Time Out, on two occasions using it to shift into the structure of the Speaker/Listener Technique, rather than to just achieve distance. Now that they were consolidating some of these techniques, the therapist moved to more skill building.

The therapist introduced Art and Pam to the structured problem-solving model taught in Christian PREP and led them through the steps on a specific problem they faced that coming week: how to handle an invitation to dinner at her parents', which neither wanted to accept for a variety of reasons. They arrived at a solution that both were pleased with, feeling that for the first time in years they had worked as a team on a problem with her parents.

Sessions 6–15: Going Deeper

Over the next ten sessions, the therapist introduced Pam and Art to the remainder of the content of Christian PREP. What follows is a sampling of what they experienced.

Issues and events model. In this model, couples are taught two essential truths: (a) day-to-day events trigger issues, which in turn cause damaging conflicts, mostly because couples do not take the time to deal with issues proactively and (b) deeper, often hidden, issues drive the greatest conflicts and frustrations of marriage. The former topic helped Pam and Art understand the importance of the various Ground Rules stressed in Christian PREP (e.g., the need for regular meetings to deal with specific issues proactively). The latter topic helped them understand the ways in which their conflicts reflected deeply seated issues that they rarely talked about constructively (e.g., power and control, caring, recognition, integrity, commitment, and the most central issue of all, acceptance and fear of rejection). Signs of hidden issues include fighting over trivial issues, having the same fight over and over, and keeping score. By considering this model, Pam and Art better understood how the conflict-management skills were crucial for them to get to the deeper issues between them.

Expectations and families of origin. Pam and Art's families set them up for very different expectations about relationships, marriage, communication, roles, personality styles, and so forth. As with too many couples, Art and Pam's differences in expectations were never understood or expressed, leading over the years to disappointments and distortions. To help Pam and Art bring these differences to light, the therapist gave them workbook assignments to help them clarify expectations. Both worked to identify (and evaluate) their expectations in many areas and, then, to share these expectations with one another.

While research shows that spouses with different faith traditions have greater risks of marital failure, Art and Pam learned that discussing such differences openly was a far wiser strategy than ignoring them. These talks about expectations became grist for some of the most deeply intimate, spiritual discussions they had ever had. What had been areas of great potential conflict and fear of rejection became the themes of their greatest connection.

Forgiveness. As they were consolidating their skills for dealing with deeper issues, Pam and Art also learned practical steps for working through forgiveness. Using the structural model, Art and Pam tackled the residual angers and grief about the affair, which had never been dealt with directly. By this point, Pam and Art had lost most of their fear and were relating with a degree of openness and trust neither had thought possible. They were in revival in their marriage and had newly found spiritual joy.

Preservation. As Art and Pam were making substantial gains, they moved into other key topics of Christian PREP with a view to learning how to preserve and protect their deepening bond in terms of commitment, friendship, fun, sensuality, and spiritual oneness.

Task 2
Create a dialogue between the counselor and the couple (or one spouse, if you prefer) showing how you might deal with communication difficulties.

When Art and Pam came to the fourth session so upset, the therapist saw this as an opportunity to demonstrate the value of structure for creating safer communication and really connecting. Here is a small sample of how the conversation from that session might have proceeded.

Therapist: OK, we've agreed to try that talk again, but this time engaging the rules of the Speaker/Listener Technique. I'm going to really press both of you to do just that. Art, why don't you take the floor first since you had raised the concern. [*Art picks up the "floor," which is a piece of card-stock on which the rules for the technique are printed. See p. 145.*]

Art: (speaker) OK. [*pause, hard swallow*] Pam, it's been my concern for years now that when we make love, your interest or response just doesn't seem to be there like it used to be.

Pam: (listener) [*quickly angry, interrupting*] What in the world do you expect? You've been treating me like crap—

Therapist: [*jumping in, hand up like a traffic cop, interrupting Pam*] Pam, hold on a second. I know you're very

153

angry and hurt, but I'm going to hold you to these rules. You'll get your chance. I know this is hard, but right now I want you to paraphrase what Art said.

Pam: (listener) [*big inhale, exhale, with visible frustration, looking at the therapist*] OK, so he said—

Therapist: [*gently, but firmly, to Pam*] Talk to him, not to me.

Pam: (listener) [*sigh, turning toward Art*] OK, so you have been bugged for a long time about me not being as responsive sexually.

Therapist: [*to Art*] Is that what you meant to say?

Art: (speaker) Yep, that's it.

Therapist: [*to Pam*] Good job. [*to Art*] Continue.

Art: (speaker) It really hurts me that we aren't connected like we used to be. I can tell you just aren't interested in being with me like you used to be. [*Pam has a sneer on her face.*]

Therapist: Pam, while you aren't interrupting, you are saying so many things with your face. I want you to try to wait until you have the floor to speak your mind. Art, I want you to try that statement again, but leave out the part about Pam's not being interested. You can't read her mind. Try telling her what *you* observe or feel. That will make it easier for her to listen to you.

Art: (speaker) [*nodding understanding*] I guess [*pause*], I guess I've really been hurting. I feel awful that when we make love we aren't able to connect like we used to. I felt so close to you then, in the past.

Pam: (listener) [*visibly softening*] You're really hurt and sad about us not being connected like we used to be.

Art: (speaker) Yes. [*looking more vulnerable*] It's not just about sex, either; it's that we don't have that sense of closeness. When we used to make love, I felt like I was so close to you that . . . I don't know.

Pam: (listener) So this isn't just about sex, it's about feeling close, and that meant a lot to you.

Art : (speaker) Exactly. I used to think, "Yeah, we have problems, but we love each other and we can count on each other." We've lost that, I think, and it's so noticeable to me when we make love because I'm not sure you're even there sometimes.

Pam: (listener) So the distance that's there when we make love really affects you in some bigger way—like we're no longer a team? [*a little tentatively*]

Art: (speaker) Yeah, like I lost my best friend. I did lose my best friend.

Pam: (listener) Me, too. You feel we lost something really important with all we have been through.

Therapist: You two are getting the hang of this, now. Good time to pass the floor? [*Art passes the floor to Pam.*]

Pam: (speaker) When you first started talking, I felt you were blaming me for "us" losing something, and I just don't think that I'm to blame for what's happening to us.

Art: (listener) [*bristling, taking a deep breath*] You seem to think it's all my fault—

Therapist: [*gently interrupting*] Time out a second. That's not a paraphrase.

Art: (listener) [*edge in his voice*] But I feel like she's saying it's all my fault.

Therapist: [*firm, still gentle demeanor*] OK, what I want you to do is to paraphrase, but in a way that gives her room to explain what she's thinking. Don't assume you got the right message.

Art: (listener) OK. You're saying you don't think you are to blame, but [*slowly, tentatively*] you think I am?

Therapist: That's the way.

Pam: (speaker) No, that's not it at all. I think *we* are to blame, that *we* really have screwed up letting things get this far. And I feel really [*tearing up*] sad.

Art : (listener) [*relaxing a great deal*] You're really sad, too, about what we've lost, and you think we've screwed it up big time.

Christian Marital Counseling

Therapist: Great job, both of you. See how you clarified this critical point by staying in the structure? If you weren't following the rules, you'd have just flared into a huge argument.

Art: That's for sure.

Therapist: Let's keep going. You're doing great.

Pam: (speaker) I've been very sensitive to the issues about sex. I know I don't respond like I used to, but I think it's because we aren't close like we used to be. While it took us awhile to get there, I really did like our lovemaking a lot—as long as I felt close to you.

Art: (listener) So, while it took us awhile to adjust, you did like it before, and it made all the difference in the world if you felt close to me in other ways.

Pam: (speaker) Yes, that's it. Sex was just one part of being close that was really good. That's what I really want back.

Their conversation continued for some time, touching on other issues such as the hard times they had with infertility, their mutual sense of loss, and the feelings Art has had that Pam is angry at him for his sterility. They drew closer, with the therapist's needing to be less and less active.

Summary

The sample dialogue illustrates several keys about the PREP approach. First, while not all couples have deep conversations this quickly, many couples will if they accept the rules and lower their defenses. Art and Pam had such strong destructive patterns that early in the counseling the therapist would have had to "sit on them" quite a bit to get them to stay with the structure. Many couples benefit enormously when we hold them accountable to the process. We are asking them, in effect, to take very seriously the simple words of Jesus: "Do to others as you would have them do to you" (Luke 6:31 NIV).

We stress that we would not want couples to communicate this way during everyday, more relaxed conversations. This is a brute-force way to bring about safe behavior so as to get at deep, painful issues. While such techniques may seem superficial, increasing safety can rapidly permit the emergence of the more important, hidden, and painful issues and feelings. If it's not minimally safe, the more vulnerable feelings of loss and longing will either not be expressed or will be expressed under the self-protective cloak of anger.

While there are many ways to intervene with couples, both Scripture and research make clear the need to find effective ways to help couples overcome the fears and get rid of the fig leaves. While we cannot get back into the garden in this lifetime, we have a loving Lord who teaches us the power of love in action as we seek to bring down the barriers to intimacy and oneness.

References

Baucom, D., and N. Epstein. 1990. *Cognitive behavioral marital therapy*. New York: Brunner/Mazel.

Johnson, D. J., and C. E. Rusbult. 1989. Resisting temptation: Devaluation of alternative partners as a means of maintaining commitment in close relationships. *Journal of Personality and Social Psychology* 57:967–80.

Markman, H. J., and K. Hahlweg. 1993. The prediction and prevention of marital distress: An international perspective. *Clinical Psychology Review* 13:29–43.

Markman, H. J., F. J. Floyd, S. M. Stanley, and H. Lewis. 1986. Prevention. In *Clinical handbook of marital therapy*, edited by N. Jacobson and A. Gurman, 173–96. New York: Guilford.

Markman, H. J., M. J. Renick, F. J. Floyd, S. M. Stanley, and M. Clements. 1993. Preventing marital distress through communication and conflict management training: A 4- and 5-year follow-up. *Journal of Consulting and Clinical Psychology* 61:1–8.

Markman, H. J., S. M. Stanley, and S. L. Blumberg. 1992. *Fighting for your marriage: The PREP approach*. Denver: PREP Educational Videos. Audiotapes.

———. 1994. *Fighting for your marriage: Positive steps for a loving and lasting relationship*. San Francisco: Jossey-Bass.

Stanley, S. M., and H. J. Markman. 1991. Relationship commitment: New kid on the cognitive block. Paper presented at the annual meeting of the Association for the Advancement of Behavior Therapy, November, New York.

———. 1992. Assessing commitment in personal relationships. *Journal of Marriage and the Family* 54:595–608.

Stanley, S. M., H. J. Markman, and S. L. Blumberg. 1991, 1994. *Fighting for your marriage: The PREP approach*. Denver: PREP Educational Videos, Inc. Videocassettes.

Stanley, S. M., H. J. Markman, M. St. Peters, and D. Leber. 1995. Strengthening marriages and preventing divorce: New directions in prevention research. *Family Relations* 44:392–401.

Stanley, S. M., and D. W. Trathen. 1994. Christian PREP: An empirically based model for marital and premarital intervention. *The Journal of Psychology and Christianity* 13:158–65.

Stanley, S. M., D. W. Trathen, and S. McCain. 1992. *Christian PREP leader's, consultant's, and couple's manuals: Prevention and Relationship Enhancement Program*. Denver: Christian PREP.

Trathen, D. W. 1995. A comparison of the effectiveness of two Christian premarital counseling programs: "Skills and information-based" utilized by Evangelical Protestant churches. Ph.D. diss., University of Denver.

Additional Resources

Training Workshops: Workshops for training in either Christian PREP or PREP are given throughout the year in Denver, Colorado. To be placed on the mailing list for information about these training opportunities, or to receive information about the *Fighting for Your Marriage* video or audiotapes, please send your name and address to Christian PREP, Inc., P.O. Box 102530, Denver, Colorado 80250-2530. Or call 303-759-9931.

Marriage Counseling

A Brief Strategic Approach to Promote Love, Faith, and Work

Everett L. Worthington Jr.

Question 1
What are the basics of your theory of marriage counseling? In your description, include your view of the typical cause(s) of marital problems and the typical goals of counseling.

Marital problems arise due to failures in carrying out God's plan for Christian discipleship. In Galatians 5:6 (RSV), Paul writes, "For in Christ Jesus neither circumcision nor uncircumcision is of any avail, but faith working through love." The Lord wants all Christians to disciple each other by this pattern—faith working through love. God especially wants marriage partners to make each other stronger disciples. Marriage mirrors God's relationship with Israel and Jesus' relationship with the church. Like our relationship with God, our relationship with our partner requires each element of the Christian pattern of discipleship: love, work, and faith. Difficulties in marriage, indeed in any relationship, are directly due to difficulties in one or more of these elements.

Definitions

Love is defined as choosing to value the partner and choosing not to devalue him or her. When partners fail to value—that is, fail to affirm, encourage, comfort, praise, admire, respect, spend time with, share intimacy with, communicate with, respectfully negotiate differences with, think the best of, and remain committed to—the spouse, then love is not being lived and marital problems can be expected. Similarly, when people actively devalue—that is, put down, belittle, discourage, irritate, criticize, become disgusted with, lose respect for, ignore, remain distant from, talk *at* (not *to*), impose solutions on, think the worst of, betray the confidence of, and demonstrate lack of commitment to—the spouse, then love suffers and marital problems can be expected.

Work is required for a good marriage. The second law of thermodynamics states a law of nature: Unless work (energy) is put into a system, the system will run downhill. For example, gardens left untended grow weeds, not vegetables. Work makes a garden prettier, more productive, and healthier. Work pulls weeds that compete with the vegetables for nourishment. Work repairs the damage of torrential rain or of a child who runs through the garden unwittingly or maliciously trampling the plants. Similarly, marriages not blessed by work degenerate. Work makes a good marriage better and repairs the damage in traumatized relationships.

"Faith is the assurance of things hoped for, the conviction of things not seen" (Heb. 11:1 RSV). When a couple pour love and work into their marriage, they don't always see the fruits immediately. They must keep faith. By investing love and work, they will eventually obtain a return. People routinely put money in a bank having faith that they will eventually obtain a return. God is infinitely more reliable than any bank. Faith is needed in four realms. First, faith in the Lord as Savior of each partner calls people into the same heavenly kingdom and unites them as brother and sister with a common heavenly Father. Second, faith in God to work his will with the marriage, which is a mysterious parallel of God's relationship with us and each partner's relationship to the other, frees a partner from grasping at control over the spouse by focusing on God's ultimate control. Third, faith in God's promises to bless us through our partner can free a spouse to receive from his or her partner something that might previously have been stubbornly blocked. Fourth, faith in counseling from a godly counselor who will help the couple try to align their will with God's can leave the couple receptive to trying new behaviors that can free them from the quagmire of negative and bitter emotions.

A Vision of Faith, Work, and Love

Faith, work, and love are the elements of a vision of marriage that is needed if the couple is to solve their marital problems and become closer to each other and to God. The vision of marriage is crucial to how partners behave in the marriage. People create a vision of marriage by weaving together threads from many sources. Most threads were copied from the parents in the family of origin. People either duplicate the patterns of or react in opposition to the adults who primarily reared them. However, other threads were plucked from observations of friends, previous dates, movies, novels, and the Bible. As the counselor becomes more important to the troubled couple, the counselor can help focus the couple's vision and even introduce them to new ways of seeing their relationship—specifically viewing it as an arena for faith working through love.

The Balm That Heals Hurts

Confession and forgiveness must be at the center of every successful marriage. Each partner in even the best marriage sins against the spouse at times. Good marriages are based on the mutual willingness of spouses to confess their own failings in sincerity and repentance. Then, the partner must forgive the injury. The calluses on the soul may be thick and hard after years of hurting without confession, repentance, or forgiveness. The counselor is a blistering agent, focusing each partner away from the spouse's failings and onto his or her own failings. Over time, confession is stimulated, blistering off a tough layer of skin. Repentance removes yet another callus. Faithful adherence to repentance takes off layer after layer of tough skin until the partner can see the tender new skin beneath the callus and can forgive.

Faith working through love is more important (and more difficult) in confession and forgiveness than in any other marital task. As the vision of marriage is acted out, confession and forgiveness are needed in each of four areas of marriage: intimacy-distance, communication, conflict resolution, and causal attributions for difficulties.

Living the Vision in Faith, Work, and Love

From the time that the baby crawls away from his or her mother but rapidly retreats to the safety of her skirt at the slightest noise, each person struggles to establish and maintain a balance of distance from and closeness to others. People's visions of marriage, their histories, and the mutation of their marital relationship as problems grow conspire to create problems in intimacy and distance. Sexual difficulties and disagreements about emotional closeness are two common marital problems. Safe but uncomfortable distance is maintained by problems in love (failing to value or actively devaluing), failure to work through the safe distance to more intimacy, and failure to have faith that changes can and will occur.

Communication is talking and listening to what is said and what is not said. It is any way of transmitting an idea from one mind to another. Unfortunately, difficulties in faith, work, or love can distort or block communication. Warped faith in the marriage or in God's role in the marriage—negative expectations—can twist understanding of behaviors, emotions, and motives; it can block communication that should occur and open the floodgates when communication should be restrained. Failure to work on improving communication can allow bad habits to be maintained. Failure to love can result in devaluing communication and in failing to value.

Conflict in marriage is inevitable, though some couples disagree more than do others. "As iron sharpens iron, so one [person] sharpens another," says Proverbs 27:17 (NIV). However, iron does not sharpen iron when swords cross in anger. They dull each other by whanging and clanging away in cuts at the head and the heart. Rather, iron sharpens iron when both are in the heat of the furnace and rub against each other purposefully to bring the blade to an edge. Differences must be resolved with a common purpose of agreeing, which transcends the individual purposes of "winning a conflict." The counselor is pivotal in helping form this vision of conflict in a troubled couple who have usually majored in thrusting at each other's vulnerable spots. Bringing about the vision and teaching practical conflict-resolution skills is faith working through love.

People instinctively seem to know what causes them to act hatefully toward their partner: It is their partner. Although today's couples are too psychologically sophisticated to admit that they almost completely blame the partner for their marital problems, most partners do blame each other for their problems. The counselor helps each person see that love demands that he or she lay aside blame and bring an honest admission of his or her own failings before God, who can raise up the partners when they come contritely to the Lord.

Commitment—The Glue That Keeps Partners Working in Faith and Love

Finally, faith working through love shows up in commitment— to God, to the partner, and to counseling. Commitment to God often flags during marital difficulties. Pain focuses people's attention on themselves. When people are in emotional pain over their marriage, they often focus solely on themselves and forget about seeking God's voice in their difficulties. The counselor reminds the people to "seek first his [God's] kingdom and his righteousness, and all these things [including marital happiness] shall be yours as well" (Matt. 6:33 RSV). Commitment to the partner has almost always eroded during marital difficulties. Commitment depends on marital satisfaction, and marital difficulties create dissatisfaction. Affairs erode both partners' faith in the marriage and cause lasting scars. Commitment to counseling is helpful if the couple is to work on their problems. Couples often enter counseling with the unrealistic belief that a few sessions will set a troubled marriage right. The typical progress of marriage counseling, though, is like a roller coaster. It has its ups and downs but usually ends at a more stable destination than when it was at the peak of disturbance. In the middle of counseling, when things do not seem to be improving for a couple, it is easy for partners to lose their commitment to counseling. If they stick with it, though, things often are improved by the journey's end.

The goals of Christian marriage counseling are to promote a pattern of faith working through love that permeates each area of the marriage: the vision, confession and forgiveness, intimacy-distance, communication, conflict management, causal attribution, and commitment. Thus, the Christian counselor seeks to help couples grow personally, maritally, and spiritually through helping them solve their marital problems. The counselor's emphasis depends on the context. A pastor who counsels or a lay counselor would focus more on Christian growth than on marital problem solving. Not only is this expected by the couple, but a pastor may not have the time nor expertise to help solve problems as thoroughly as the professional counselor. On the other hand, couples expect professional counselors to help solve problems. They expect less promotion of spiritual and personal growth. While I believe that both problem solving and promoting spiritual and personal growth are goals for any Christian counseling, the emphasis differs.

Regardless of the setting—lay, pastoral, or professional—the couple should leave counseling recognizing that their calling as Christian partners is mutual discipleship through faith working through love.

Question 2
For what kind of people is your approach most appropriate?

I have used my approach mostly as marital counseling in which one professional counselor works conjointly with a couple. As with any marital counseling, it is not always possible to see spouses conjointly, so occasionally I have counseled individuals. For premarital counseling and marital enrichment, I have used the approach with groups.

The approach of promoting faith working through love is flexible and can be applied in a variety of settings. With professional counseling (see Worthington 1989), I assess the couple for three sessions and follow assessment with six to twelve counseling sessions, depending on the results of the assessment. For pastoral counseling (see Worthington and McMurry 1994), the approach uses five sessions, the first of which is assessment. Friendship or lay counseling (see Worthington 1994) can be structured to fit the relationship between friends. In premarital counseling (see Worthington 1991), I apply the model more educationally, rather than therapeutically, depending on the couple's maturity and experience together.

The principles of faith working through love are universal, and I have used them with Christians and non-Christians. Most couples receive the ideas and use them. With couples who are hostile to Christianity, I inform them early in counseling of my values to afford them the opportunity to seek a referral to another counselor or, if they stick with me, to allow them to make informed decisions about the merit of my counsel. Naturally, I do not think it is moral, ethical, or in line with Christianity to try to coerce or force a faith in Jesus on people who do not believe. However, neither do I believe it is moral, ethical, or Christian to pretend that I can counsel people without my values influencing my behavior. Thus, when I use this counseling approach, I alert couples to my values and beliefs as they become pertinent to counseling.

Question 3
What are your foci for counseling?

The personal relationship between counselor and client is paramount. Humans were created by God for both human agency and relationships, which mirrors the essence of the Trinity. Counseling is discipleship in which the counselor is discipled by God to apply faith working through love despite the counselor's frustrations when working with couples. The counselor disciples the couple, promoting faith where there is hopelessness, work where there is powerlessness, and love where there is rejection.

Early in my counseling, I was enamored by active marital therapies—(a) cognitive-behavioral, (b) structural (Minuchin), and (c) strategic (Haley and Madanes). Each theory emphasized problem solving. Many techniques from these approaches to marital therapy fit my easygoing style, in which I helped people solve problems and feel less pain. However, since 1987 or 1988, I have come to appreciate a more empathic, person-centered style. I see more truth to psychoanalytic notions of unconsciously motivated behavior, and I read and practice some of the techniques of emotion-focused marital therapy (Greenberg and Johnson 1988). My approach does not emphasize behavior, cognition, and structure as much as it did. Now, I try harder to create an emotional climate that facilitates the revival of positive emotions and productive vision for marriage. In short, I try to promote faith, work, and love through my counseling. I want to promote faith like a pastor; promote work like a cognitive-behavioral, structural, or strategic marital therapist; and promote love like Jesus.

Whereas my early writings acknowledged that people are whole, interconnected beings, my counseling sometimes treated them more like stick figures with big heads and anemic bodies that were too emaciated to hold emotions and unconscious motives. I still agree with my earlier writings—people are complex combinations of emotions, cognitions, behaviors, somas (physical bodies), and spirits who are intimately attached to their social and physical environments (see Worthington 1982)—and I have tried to bring my behavior during counseling more in line with that picture of human nature.

Question 4
How is your marriage counseling conducted?

Effective marital counseling is based on accurate assessment. This is true in self-help, friendship counseling, pastoral counseling, and professional counseling. If we do not know what the problem is, we will not treat it effectively.

Most marital counseling is time limited. The time limits vary (perhaps only hours for friends, five sessions for pastors, or three assessment and up to twelve therapy sessions for professionals), but progress often is made more quickly when people have a clear target at which to aim. When time limits are set, many couples have similar experiences as they move through counseling. Initial optimism often gives way to some discouragement when a couple find that an instant cure is unlikely. However, after the couple resolve to work on the marriage, progress resumes. With progress comes lifted spirits. When inevitable setbacks occur, the couple doubt their progress, question the wisdom of continuing counseling, and become tempted to fall back into old patterns or simply end the marriage. But if the partners work through the "dark night" of marriage counseling, they can see the dawn. The couple can move to higher levels of faith and love. Some couples go through several such cycles of relapse and revitalization, of the cross and the resurrection. At the agreed-upon final session, most couples are ready to end counseling.

Counseling is an adventure. In the beginning, the counselor joins the couple in a journey through a potentially dangerous land. After assessing the couple's needs, the counselor acts as a guide, pointing out where hidden dangers lie and helping the couple find the object of their hunt. During this time, old hunting habits must be broken and new ones formed. Importantly, new habits cannot be taught directly. Most couples behave so habitually that although they have learned new behaviors, they do not use them—unless the old patterns are identified, disrupted, and eventually destroyed. Once the new behaviors begin to be used, the couple is helped to consolidate those patterns into their permanent repertoire. At last, they can use the patterns well enough that they no longer need the counselor.

The counselor must be active throughout counseling, interrupting toxic exchanges and directing couples in how to interact productively. This does not imply that the counselor does not allow the expression of anger, fear, pain, sadness, or other negative emotions. Rather, the counselor helps the couple communicate those emotions in ways that show love—valuing and not devaluing the partner—faith, and work.

I employ guided self-discovery more than teaching, though at times direct teaching is helpful. After times of self-discovery, I may summarize what the couple learned, or I may ask the couple to summarize. Thus, teaching is important, but *telling* couples truths is rarer than helping them interact so they can *learn* truth and then summarizing their learning.

I allow little spontaneous argument, but I often direct couples to discuss things with each other. It is easy to feel overwhelmed by the anger and passion of a highly conflicted couple who have argued heatedly for years and can fight viciously during counseling. I try to prevent hurtful arguments; instead, I coach the couple to disagree in love—continuing to value each other throughout.

Question 5
How do you deal with a few of the common marital problems?

Intimacy

Several problems primarily involve intimacy: the withdrawn spouse, the emotional distancer-pursuer pattern, and sexual difficulties. Each problem shares a common root: disturbance in faith working through love. The counselor must assess the degree to which the problem is one of faith, work, or love (not valuing or devaluing) and then build a heartfelt desire in the partners to live the Christian pattern of faith working through love.

The withdrawn spouse has emotionally, and sometimes physically, left the relationship. Perhaps he or she works on a hobby or sport to the exclusion of the mate. Perhaps he or she spends seventy hours at work each week. By withdrawing, the partner has communicated (a) that he or she lacks faith in the marriage, (b) that work on the relationship has ceased, and (c) that he or she does not value, or actively devalues, the spouse.

I begin by discussing ways that people in general meet their needs for intimacy, aloneness, and coactive time. I have the couple analyze their time schedules in terms of how each activity contributes to meeting needs for intimacy, aloneness, or coaction. I explore whether each spouse perceives his or her needs as being met by the way he or she is using time. Each spouse discusses—in the context of wanting to show love to the partner—whether there are other activities that could meet his or her needs and simultaneously contribute to better meeting the spouse's needs. Compromises are proposed—with the justification that the partners must work hard to forge a new pattern of living—and each partner undertakes a single modification of the time schedule that might contribute to more harmony while still meeting needs for intimacy, aloneness, and coaction. An appeal is made to maintain the faith that God will provide a way to work out the difficulties. Often making a single modification in each person's schedule will lead to other changes.

The emotional distancer-pursuer pattern involves a spouse who demands intimacy (the pursuer) and another who avoids intimacy (the distancer). In the later stages, the pursuer tires of the chase, withdraws, and criticizes the distancer. The distancer quickly recognizes that the pursuer is no longer pursuing and returns to a moderate distance, where, barraged by criticisms, the distancer fights back.

If a counselor tries to promote additional intimacy between the partners, the distancer perceives the counselor as being an emotional pursuer, like the partner, and the distancer may resist the counselor's efforts to promote intimacy. With emotional distancer-pursuer couples, I use an intervention that I call "sealed orders." Prior to the session, I prepare two sealed envelopes, each with directives—one to the distancer, one to the pursuer. In the session, we discuss intimacy, and I describe the distancer-pursuer pattern. After the partners have elaborated the pattern, I summarize it using a chart that I prepared earlier. I suggest that others have experienced and dealt with the distancer-pursuer pattern, and I question whether they have the faith and are willing to work hard to change their behavior for a week. When they agree, I give each a sealed envelope. The pursuer's envelope directs the pursuer to refrain from requesting closeness and to avoid criticizing the spouse either verbally or mentally. If the pursuer criticizes the distancer, even in thought, the pursuer must pray that the Lord will help her or him refrain from such criticism and, if the pursuer feels it is warranted, the pursuer should ask for forgiveness for criticizing. The distancer must think of a way that he or she can show the partner that the partner is valued. The activity is completely up to the distancer, but it should be an activity that the pursuer enjoys and one that builds a feeling of closeness between partners. The last part of each directive states that neither partner is allowed to tell his or her orders to the other, but by the following session, each partner should be able to guess correctly the other's orders.

I treat sexual difficulties with a modified cognitive-behavioral approach, first determining the degree to which the problem is physical, individually psychological, and/or attributable to the couple's interactions—both throughout the day and in the bedroom. The couple and I discuss the difficulties in detail. This is sometimes difficult with conservative Christians, who may feel that their sexual relationship is intensely private. However, if I treat sex as a natural part of marriage and a natural topic of discussion in counseling (assuming there are difficulties in the sexual area), then partners also usually treat sex more matter-of-factly.

I comment that they seem to want to show love to each other and that God intended married couples to have a pleasing sexual relationship. I try to deal with their difficulty, once it has been discussed, with a combination of permission giving (i.e., exposing inappropriate sexual taboos), communication training, sensate focus, and specific sex therapy techniques. More than most areas of marriage, the sexual relationship is an area for showing love by valuing the partner's vulnerabilities, having faith in the face of frustrating difficulties, and working toward a mutually pleasurable relationship.

Communication and Conflict Management

Most of the communication and conflict-management techniques I use have been taken from other therapists' theories. For example, I draw heavily from John Gottman's work on leveling and editing, preventing poor communication, and promoting controlled communication of affect (Gottman 1993). I teach the difference between the intent of the communicator and the impact of the communication. I use Roger Fisher and William Ury's (1981) *Getting to Yes: Negotiating Agreement without Giving In* to help people identify the interests behind the intractable positions they stake out in conflicts. I try to control the intensity of the conflict or inhibit an especially verbally dominant partner by providing a single object—I use a tennis ball—to signify whose turn it is to talk.

Promoting Positive Feelings

Drawing on Salvador Minuchin's theorizing (Minuchin and Fishman 1981), I use physical space in the office as a metaphor for emotional closeness. I ask partners to pretend that the distance across the room represents the amount of emotional closeness or distance they feel, from standing against opposite walls as the ultimate separateness and hugging as the ultimate emotional closeness. After clients move to a distance that both feel represents their current emotional state, I have them move to a distance that represents their ideal. Often emotional distancer-pursuer patterns become graphic at that phase because the distancer usually wants more space than does the pursuer. Most couples, though, hug. I ask if they think the ideal is achievable. Usually, they do not, so I have them position themselves at a "practical ideal." Finally, I have them pull their chairs to the distance apart that they currently feel they are.

I ask partners to talk to each other in a way that they feel can get them closer. If they lapse into negative talk or criticism, I suggest other ways to get closer, such as talking about pleasant memories, their dreams as a couple, the joy their children bring them, or other agreeable topics. At various times, I ask how close they are feeling, and the partners move their chairs to signify the increasing closeness. At the end of the session, I summarize what they have learned throughout the session: they can affect their feelings of intimacy through their choice of topics and through the ways they discuss topics.

Confession and Forgiveness

All marriage partners hurt each other at times, so forgiveness is crucial to any lasting satisfactory marriage. Usually, partners in turmoil focus on their own hurts and the need of forgiveness by their partner. Both partners need forgiveness, so both are right in thinking that their partners should seek forgiveness, but being right does not help their marriage. In fact, to help the marriage, both partners need to focus on *seeking*, not granting, forgiveness. By searching their own hearts for their sins against their partners, then confessing their sins and repenting (turning away) from them, spouses develop a more empathic understanding of their partners and consequently demand less from their partners.

I conduct a forgiveness session near the end of therapy. Partners are told to consider, during the week between sessions, how they have hurt the other in their recent past. At the following session, they each confess those hurtful behaviors. Each partner is coached to listen to the spouse's confessions but not to offer instant forgiveness. Usually, despite warnings not to forgive rapidly, partners spontaneously forgive each other. Crying is common as partners see each other making themselves vulnerable, sometimes for the first time in years. Mutual confession and forgiveness are healing.

Commitment

At the end of marital counseling, a ritual is often helpful to solidify the commitment that was initially made to the marriage into a recommitment to renew love. Joshua made a monument to the Lord after leading the Israelites into the Promised Land (finally). I encourage couples to design their own Joshua monument. Any ritual can be used as a regular reminder to the couple of what the Lord has done for them throughout marriage counseling—making them more effective disciples of Christ who live out faith working through love.

Task 1
Respond to the case study by telling precisely how you might typically treat it, in how many sessions, in what order, and with what responses by the clients throughout counseling. One restriction: Assume that between the third and fourth counseling sessions with you— regardless of what had gone on during the previous session—the couple had a major argument and come to the fourth session in some crisis.

I might counsel Art and Pam differently depending on a careful assessment of their relationship and on whether I was doing pastoral or professional counseling. With pastoral counseling, I would use a five-session strategy (including assessment and counseling) that conceptualizes the problem and solution similarly to the longer-duration professional counseling. Professional marital counseling might entail as many as three assessment sessions plus about ten counseling sessions, but in the mid-1990s and beyond, it would usually be *brief* marital therapy of one two-hour assessment session and from five to eight counseling sessions.

In pastoral counseling, I would pay more attention to each partner's spiritual life and set less ambitious goals for changing Art and Pam's marriage relative to professional counseling. Leaving you to pursue the pastoral model through other reading (Worthington and McMurry 1994), I will describe brief marital therapy with this couple—one assessment session plus eight counseling sessions.

Assessment: Conceptualizing the Main Problem

Faith working through love. As I have discovered by meeting with Art and Pam for two hours in a single assessment session and having them complete the Couple's PreCounseling Inventory and the Personal Assessment of Intimacy in Relationships (see Additional Resources on p. 185), Pam and Art are having problems mainly because they are failing in faith working through love. Their main deficit is in love, but weaknesses in work and faith aggravate the problem. By the end of the assessment session, I will present a verbal account of their strengths and weaknesses, a conceptualization of the major targets for counseling, and a suggested number of counseling sessions to achieve specific goals. If we agree to work together, counseling will begin in the following session with a presentation to Art and Pam of a written account of my assessment.

Supporting evidence for the conceptualization. Art and Pam daily fall down in love. They bicker and fight, continually devaluing each other. At times, poison erupts in a spew of yelling and cursing. They verbally batter and cut one another, trying to erode a sense of value that they once held for each other. Whereas they blessed and valued each other in their early years of marriage, they now fail to edify and value one another. Thus, not only do they poison each other with devaluing, they also starve one another of the needed nourishment of valuing love. This assessment contributes to treatment even though Art and Pam have not agreed to begin counseling. I strive to help Art and Pam see the beauty of the love they fail to practice, but could practice once again. Both a sense of failure to love and a vision of the love they wish to have are necessary for Art and Pam to rediscover the smorgasbord of love they can feast upon.

The couple's devaluing has been constant since the beginning of their fifth year of marriage. Pam was fired from her job and Art is sterile, occurrences that provided both with a concrete sense of loss of value. Both feeling of low value, they were unable to turn to the Lord and draw esteem from him. Both experienced blows almost simultaneously, and each became lost in the vanity of his or her own inadequacies.

Conflict erupted and an affair flamed, leaving a burned-out relationship and two hollow partners, professing forgiveness but showing little evidence of it. Attempts at intimacy—sexual and emotional—were "irritating," though they had not been so when the relationship was based on love and value. Art and Pam's dance of intimacy and distance, of demands and counterdemands, took on a more symbolic role as an issue that each could use to try to vainly assert his or her power—to no avail. Now their marriage is characterized by feelings of lack of value, attempts to gain esteem through winning the power struggle, chronic niggling conflict, poor communication, blame, failure to accept responsibility for one's own part in the difficulties, and a general loss of vitality (life and energy) in the marriage.

Their need: intervention of the living God. Art and Pam's love is at a crucial point—almost extinguished. They need the breath of God to fan it ablaze and set them working to fuel the fire. Yet, faith is in short supply. Each partner seems to have a saving faith in Jesus, but both have lost faith that their relationship can flourish, so their efforts at restoring the marriage are minimal. They have lost faith *working through* love (see Gal. 5:6). Their faith is brittle straw, kept apart from the fire of the Holy Spirit, who wants to work through love in their marriage to ignite the straw. Pam and Art confine their faith to church and do not allow it into the marriage. Held together by a fragile commitment, they need a renewing, revitalized love that shows that their faith has spread, through work, into their marriage.

175

As their counselor, I must try to be one of God's prods to stir up Art and Pam to faith and good works.

Eight Counseling Sessions

Art and Pam will have little success building intimacy and increasing love until they are able to talk about some of the power struggles and to communicate differently. Thus, the counseling must begin with conflict resolution. Importantly, however, I do not think Art and Pam must *resolve* all their conflicts before they can build intimacy, but they must learn to talk about them differently—in a way that conveys valuing and eschews devaluing. They must stick with efforts to communicate value even though such efforts are difficult and may often fail. By dealing with disagreements first, Art and Pam begin to experience faith working through love from the beginning of treatment.

Session 1. I would present to Art and Pam the written assessment report and say that we would address *the way* they deal with conflict. Our goal is not to resolve differences but to discuss differences in love so they can resolve them over time. Art and Pam would identify a conflict of moderate proportion on which to begin.

I would teach the couple that whatever intent they have with any communication of valuing love may not necessarily be received by the partner in the intended way. They must learn, therefore, to monitor the effect that their communications are having and strive to keep the intent of their communication loving. I would have them both listen to the partner and paraphrase what they perceived the partner to say prior to their offering any rebuttal to the partner's arguments.

Session 2. After I have instructed the couple in conflict-management techniques and have them apply their learning to a conflict of moderate intensity, I would try to deal with a more emotionally powered conflict—Art's egocentrism and Pam's attempts to control. During the session, I would have two objectives: primarily to help the couple *practice* using the principle of valuing love and secondarily to help them understand blame differently.

(A portion of the conversation from this session is excerpted on pp. 181–85.)

Session 3. In this session, I would plan to deal with issues of closeness, particularly the emotional distancer-pursuer conflict. My goals would be similar to those for session 2; however, now I would want the couple to practice valuing love while understanding intimacy and distance differently.

Despite my plans for the third counseling session after the single assessment session, Art and Pam arrive in turmoil in the midst of a hot conflict. Instead of dissuading them from the conflict (because it was not the conflict *I* had suggested we work on), I would characterize their conflict as a good opportunity for them to discuss a topic that is on the front burner instead of one that is more removed from their emotions. Throughout the conflict, I would try to help the couple discuss their differences while working with them to practice not devaluing each other and to communicate value to each other.

While partners tend to think in terms of resolving their specific disagreements, I think more about the generality of helping partners communicate in ways that show that they value and love each other. To the extent that I can help the couple accept my goal for them—showing love in all situations—they will succeed at changing their marriage. To the extent that they focus on each individual conflict and its resolution, they may make small changes but will not make lasting changes that build love.

Session 4. Having come to some resolution of the crisis in the previous session, Art and Pam would be more willing to participate in changing their communication regarding intimacy. We would discuss their different needs for intimacy and distance. I would use the physical space of the office to represent emotional distance and closeness. By having them move back and forth across the office as their feelings of closeness change, I hope they would understand that (a) they have the power to become closer by valuing each other or to become more distant by devaluing each other, (b) they use different tactics to keep each other at arm's length, and (c) even if they have different needs for closeness and distance, they can use friends and other family members to help meet those needs—that is, the spouse does not have to meet all of one's needs for intimacy and distance.

Session 5. We would discuss each partner's family of origin, trying to show that much of the intimacy and distancing was learned in the family of origin, as were habitual patterns of devaluing and valuing. I would also explore the church histories of the clients. We would discuss the valuing that should be evident in the church among the adopted children of God. I would commend Art and Pam for the hard work that they had exerted thus far at showing Christian love to each other, even when dealing with emotional conflicts.

I would suggest that Art and Pam consider ways to arrange their lives to better meet their needs for intimacy, time together, and distance, and I would inquire about ways to adjust their schedules to meet each one's personal needs while considering the other. With each adjustment, I would point out how the partners are showing love through their willingness to lay down their lives for the spouse, which is the essence of valuing love. Their behavior shows a willingness to sacrifice, exert effort, and have faith that the changes will pay off. It is the essence of practical Christianity.

Sometime in the fifth, sixth, or seventh session, I would anticipate a relapse. The couple would likely have a major disagreement as they feel themselves getting closer and more intimate. As the old ways are disrupted, the partners both love and hate the change. They are ambivalent, and they need support to strengthen their desire for change. I would thus meet the relapse with a statement that I indeed anticipated it, thus characterizing the relapse as evidence that they are making progress, not as evidence that progress cannot be made. I would suggest that the relapse poses a deep challenge to them as a couple, for they are facing their own ambivalence. The challenge is nothing less than an attack on their faith. As they live out their faith through practical valuing love—even in the difficult times—that is precisely what Satan does not want. They should expect attacks, deal with the attacks to their faith by affirming the sovereignty of God, and press on to develop even more love in action.

Such reasoning is tailored to individual couples. Because Art and Pam are both conservative Christians, I use language with which they can identify. By the fifth session, I should know how to describe the relapse so that Art and Pam can accept it. Naturally, if the couple were not Christian or if only one partner were Christian, I would not frame the intervention in such starkly Christian language.

Session 6. Because Art and Pam presented the problem of an unsatisfying sexual relationship, I would explore that relationship in the sixth session. (If this were pastoral counseling, I would be more reluctant to delve into the specifics of their sexual life because the relationship between a pastor and his or her parishioners is more complex and multifaceted than one between a professional counselor and his or her clients.) I would embed any suggestions about improving Art and Pam's sexual relationship in terms of their attempting to value each other and being willing to sacrifice for each other.

Also in session 6, I would begin to discuss confession and forgiveness, crucial elements of the troubled marriage that would be addressed more completely in session 7. All healthy marriages must deal with the inevitable hurts that partners inflict on each other. In Art and Pam's marriage, there is ample evidence of past hurts. Because infidelity has occurred, I would anticipate that at least two sessions would be needed to deal with forgiveness. Thus, in session 6, we would discuss hurts associated with the affair. I would hope to engender mutual empathy through the discussion and would coach the partners to discuss the times that they hurt the other person rather than the times when they were hurt. I would also discuss whether and how each partner forgives himself or herself for having hurt the other.

Session 7. In this forgiveness session, each partner would formally confess times when he or she has hurt the other and would seek forgiveness. Art and Pam would sit facing each other and describe actions that have hurt the other person, asking for forgiveness. The partner would listen and grant forgiveness if he or she felt it.

I have described the preparation for and conduct of such a session in several sources (for example, Worthington and McMurry 1994). Generally, I would not conduct a forgiveness session unless I believed that Art and Pam (or any couple) were ready to forgive each other. The formal forgiveness session is a concrete demonstration of forgiveness in a couple who are clearly ready and willing to forgive each other. It helps the partners express what they already are beginning to feel. Like most of the interventions I prefer (e.g., writing an assessment report instead of merely conveying it verbally, actually practicing conflict-management behaviors, using videotapes of the couple's disagreements in counseling, using physical space as a metaphor for intimacy and distance, and making a Joshua memorial), this forgiveness intervention makes change very "real" by giving it a physical form that is clearly observable by both partners.

Session 8. During assessment, we had set clear goals for what we thought might be accomplished within eight sessions. For this last session, I would prepare a written report in which I summarize those goals and assess the couple's nearness to reaching them. Then I would give a copy of the report to each partner, discuss the counseling, and identify whatever goals the couple still can work on at home. If little progress has been made toward the goals, we would discuss whether to extend counseling for some agreed-upon period of time or whether the couple should work alone. Chances are good, however, that the couple will have made substantial progress, which will give me opportunities to compliment them on their courage and faith. These positive attributions are essential if Art and Pam are to maintain their changes. At the end of the session, they would create a "Joshua memorial" to celebrate their progress and form a symbolic way to remember from where they came during their wilderness experience.

The treatment I have outlined is obviously arbitrary. Art and Pam might require more, or fewer, than eight counseling sessions. Conflict management was covered in only three sessions, which might not be enough to make lasting changes. Seeing the couple as they interact allows me to judge how many sessions are needed to affect change. In the course of therapy, I base the number of sessions, the conduct of the sessions, and the content of the sessions on each particular couple.

In brief marital therapy, I present counseling to the couple not as a "cure" for marital problems but as a catalyst for change. I often describe counseling as a turning point, for the couple may not be greatly different than they were at the start of counseling, but they are moving in a completely different direction. In that way, the changes they make can be profound in the reorientation of faith, work, and love.

Task 2
Create a dialogue between the counselor and the couple (or one spouse, if you prefer) showing how you might deal with communication difficulties.

The following narrative represents a portion of what might have transpired during session 2.

Turning the videotape player on, I walked back to my seat and settled in, saying to Art and Pam, "As you remember, we're going to continue taping these sessions. Okay?" They both nod. "Last session, you discussed your disagreement over limits on visiting your parents," I said, nodding to Pam.

"Yes," Pam recalled, "and we didn't resolve anything."

"That's true," I said. "We didn't resolve the issue. You have disagreed about that issue for probably fifteen years, and I never thought you could agree in less than an hour."

"Well, I had hoped . . ." Pam let the sentence trail off.

I continued, "We probably won't be able to completely resolve any long-standing issues in a few weeks of counseling. That wouldn't be realistic. However, I hope that you learn *how* to disagree in a less hurtful, more loving way. If you can do that, *you* can resolve the tough issues over time."

Pam shifted her attention to Art and said, "We won't be able to work anything out as long as he's so selfish."

I said, "Let's think back to last week. What *did* you get out of the session?"

She pondered the question for a few seconds. "The main idea was that it's easy to misunderstand each other, and we need to listen more."

181

Art chimed in, "You showed us that our intent of communicating love to each other doesn't always have that impact on the other person."

Pam karate-chopped the air. "You just cut me off. He asked *me*, and you butted in. You're so insensitive." She turned to me. "This is typical. He's so wrapped up in impressing others, and he's so egotistical—"

"Don't start with the egotistical bull again, you controlling b—"

"—that he never thinks of—"

"You're trying to dominate the—"

"—anyone but himself."

"—conversation."

I held up both hands, saying, "Whoa. Hold on." Both Art and Pam looked at me. "It's easy to see how these arguments explode. But if you continue to argue this way, you aren't going to restore the love between you, as you each said you want to do." Art and Pam glanced at each other with both hostility and sheepishness. "I want you to deal with this issue. Pam, you claim that Art is egotistical and self-centered, and Art, you claim that Pam is controlling."

"It's not a claim. It's a fact," spat out Pam.

That was provocative—to both Art and to me—but I knew we would not progress if Pam provoked me into an argument, so I ignored the interruption. I continued, "I want to analyze this disagreement. You can benefit if you understand how this happened because you can avoid these arguments once you know how they start." I paused, looking at each of them. "First, tell me how you think this got started. Pam?"

She responded, "He interrupted me. Then he tried to talk me down."

I looked to Art. "Art?"

"That didn't start it," Art said. "I was giving a factual answer to a factual question. She got threatened because she couldn't be in control—"

"Hold it, Pam," I said, seeing that Pam was on the verge of interrupting. "I see that you want to jump in, but let me get Art's side."

"Thanks," Art said. "She gets threatened when she's not in control, and she aggressively asserts herself."

"So," I said, "you each see what the other does to provoke you to argue."

"Well," said Art, "I guess I was being a know-it-all."

"I guess you were," said Pam.

"And you, Art," I continued, "provoked Pam."

"Yeah."

I did not say anything. Pam shifted uncomfortably in the few seconds of silence before saying, "I feel like you want me to say that it was my fault, but I didn't do anything to provoke him until *after* he provoked me."

I responded, "So you think you contributed to the escalation, but you didn't start the fuss." She nodded. "Well, I'm not trying to get either of you to admit that you're to blame. I just want you each to see that you have the power to make the conflict better or worse. If you want to practice a love that values the other and doesn't devalue the other, then you'll begin to de-escalate or avoid conflict more often."

Pam said, "You're right. I want to rebuild our love. I'm tired of fighting all the time." She began to cry. "I'm tired of living in a perpetual fight."

Art reached over and rubbed Pam's shoulder in comforting circles. She sobbed loudly and buried her face in her hands.

"I'm tired of fighting, too," Art said. "I love Pam, and I want to get out of this rut." Pam reached for a tissue and wiped her dripping nose and eyes.

I said, "I can see that you are held together with bonds of love that are stronger than either of you see. I know that you want to value each other and to stop devaluing each other. Watching you, Art, comfort Pam shows me how much you care for each other. And watching you, Pam, respond to his gentle touch shows me how much you each yearn for those gentle touches." Pam sobbed again and, leaning awkwardly over the arm of the chair, buried her head against Art's chest. "Can we watch the videotape of the argument and see how it developed?" They nodded.

As I walked to the VCR, I saw Art give Pam a squeeze. Pam wiped her eyes. I rewound the tape and found a section in which I was speaking:

Worthington: . . . I hope that you learn *how* to disagree in a less hurtful, more loving way. If you can do that, *you* can resolve the tough issues over time.

Pam: We won't be able to work anything out as long as he's so selfish.

I paused the tape.

"Oh, my," said Pam. "I was kinda nasty there, wasn't I?"

"Your offhand comment devalued Art," I responded. "Let me say, however, that even though this was the first provocation in this disagreement, it doesn't mean that you *caused* the disagreement. It doesn't matter who said something *first* because someone always said something before that. What matters is that at every point, *you each* have the responsibility for how you are going to respond. You can respond in a way that values or devalues the other. It's a choice every time you say something."

I started the tape again, and we watched the following exchange.

Art: You showed us that our intent of communicating love to each other doesn't always have that impact on the other person.

Pam: You just cut me off. He asked *me*, and you butted in. You're so insensitive.

"Art, do you see that you interrupted Pam?" I asked.

"Yeah," he replied.

"How do you think she felt?"

He responded, "Really torqued off. That's easy to see."

I went on, "I think she felt devalued, as if you didn't value her enough to let her give a full explanation."

"You're right," said Pam.

"And feeling devalued, what did you do, Pam?" I asked.

"I devalued Art," said Pam. "I called him insensitive."

"So, Art, you didn't show love to Pam," I said. "You devalued her. So she responded tit-for-tat. And Pam, you didn't show love to Art, and he, too, responded tit-for-tat. If you value your mate, it will beget valuing, but if you devalue your mate, it will wipe out love." Both partners nodded. "Let's look at the next part of the tape. . . ."

References

Fisher, R., and W. Ury. 1981. *Getting to yes: Negotiating agreement without giving in.* New York: Penguin.

Gottman, J. M. 1993. A theory of marital dissolution and stability. *Journal of Family Psychology* 7:57–75.

Greenberg, L. S., and S. M. Johnson. 1988. *Emotionally focused therapy for couples.* New York: Guilford.

Minuchin, S., and H. C. Fishman. 1981. *Family therapy thechniques.* Cambridge, Mass.: Harvard University Press.

Worthington, E. L., Jr. 1982. *When someone asks for help: A practical guide for counseling.* Downers Grove, Ill.: InterVarsity.

———. 1989. *Marriage counseling: A Christian approach to counseling couples.* Downers Grove, Ill.: InterVarsity.

———. 1991. *Counseling before marriage.* Dallas: Word Books.

———. 1994. *I care about your marriage: Helping friends and families with marital problems.* Chicago: Moody.

Worthington, E. L., Jr., and D. McMurry. 1994. *Marriage conflicts: Resources for strategic pastoral counseling.* Grand Rapids: Baker.

Additional Resources

The Couple's PreCounseling Inventory by R. B. Stuart is available from Research Press, 2612 North Mattis Avenue, Champaign, Illinois 61820. Schaefer and Olson's Personal Assessment of Intimacy in Relationships is available from David H. Olson and M. T. Schaefer, Family Social Science, 290 McNeal Hall, University of Minnesota, Saint Paul, Minnesota 55108.

Marital Counseling

A Christian Integrative Approach

H. Norman Wright

Question 1
What are the basics of your theory of marriage counseling? In your description, include your view of the typical cause(s) of marital problems and the typical goals of counseling.

Hopefully the theoretical framework for my current approach to marital counseling is different from what I did in each of the past three decades. I trust it will not be the same in the future. Continued growth and improvement as a therapist are a given, and the greater the flexibility of the therapist in style and approach, the greater the effectiveness.

People Who Have Influenced Me

My own development as a marital therapist came more from seminars and literature than from the academic setting since my initial training was in individual therapy via Rogerian, Adlerian, and Gestalt therapy with minimal marital emphasis. Studying under William Glasser for an extended period of time was quite influential. This experience actually provided the basis for my primary orientation, which is referred to today as solution-oriented therapy (if one needs a descriptive term). Those who have been an influence include James Framo, Neil Jacobson, Aaron Beck, and Shirley Luthman. Three specific works having influenced me are Daniel B. Wile's *Couples Therapy* (1981), Billie Ables's *Couples in Therapy* (1977), and Richard Stuart's *Helping Couples Change* (1980). A third group of influences has come not from therapists but from teachers, theoreticians, and writers. What they have said about the marriage relationship is as important as the various therapists who present theory and structure. As the therapists emphasize the framework and approach, the others add additional content and substance.

Causes of Marital Problems

There is no one major cause of marital problems other than our sinful nature. Probably each therapist has his or her own list of the causes, but one of the most basic is neglected preparation for leaving the single lifestyle and moving into marriage. As each year passes, I am more convinced of the efficacy of individualized premarital counseling. It is not a panacea and will not resolve all the identified issues, but it helps by identifying issues and helping the couple develop problem-solving skills. In about 30 percent of the cases, we find the couples decide not to marry. Fortunately, they discover prior to marriage that the relationship is not going to work.

Some of the more prevalent causes for marital disruption are low self-esteem, inadequate or unhealthy separation from parents, lack

of awareness and understanding of gender and personality differences (which include not learning to blend or complement one
another), and the inability to relate or connect emotionally (which
creates an intimacy vacuum within a relationship). Any pathology
that an individual brings into marriage certainly impedes bonding.
Often the presenting problem is a symptom rather than the main
issue; thus, we need to consider that what the couple presents as
the issue may or may not be the core problem. We often hear in the
general press that finances are the major cause for marital difficulty,
but I have not really seen the evidence for this. Frequently financial
problems are the receptacle for other issues, such as power and control, personality differences, family-of-origin influence, and others.
The items enumerated here are just the tip of the iceberg. Each marital therapist needs to search for what is beneath the surface and be
prepared for the unexpected.

We can never ignore that there are six people in every marriage.
A parent's influence is always present in either a reactive or proactive sense. A healthy, positive role model of a husband, wife, and
marital relationship can be a negative interference in a marriage just
as much as a deficit relationship can be. A person may expect his
or her partner to be a replica of a parent. If the parental model is
repeated in the individual's marriage, unmet needs from the parental
relationship are often carried, consciously or unconsciously, into the
union. Unless confronted, these needs will interfere.

Goals of Marriage Counseling

The overall goal of marriage counseling is the healing of the marital relationship and the redefining of the interaction of the two
people so that both experience fulfillment and satisfaction. But there
are intermediate goals to be achieved along the way. Our goals, as
well as our approach, will be different if the person or couple is experiencing an immediate crisis as compared to an ongoing marital
issue.

Some clients come in a state of trauma or crisis because of the
immediacy of shattering experiences. These include discovering the
unfaithfulness of a partner, receiving news that the partner is seek-

ing divorce, experiencing physical abuse, discovering that the partner has been sexually abusing their child, or discovering pornographic material hidden by the partner. In each case, the individual is seeking help for marital issues, but because of his or her numbness and disorientation, the individual's own existence must first be stabilized. Listening, reflecting feelings, assigning simple tasks, and empathetically supporting compose the approach to reach this first-step goal (for more information on crisis counseling, see Wright 1993). Once this first-step goal has been accomplished, focusing upon the precipitating event and rebuilding the relationship can occur.

If only one party seeks counseling, one of my goals is to bring in the resistant partner. I do not subscribe to the view that if you do not have both parties you cannot work on the relationship. You can—but in a different way. However, if possible, it is important to have the other partner join as soon as possible so that he or she is not alienated by my working with one spouse. Most resistant partners will come in. There are three approaches to use. Phoning and explaining that you need his or her perspective and would be willing to meet with him or her is one option. Writing either a linear or a paradoxical letter to the nonattending spouse, as described by Allen Wilcoxon and David Fenell (1983), may also be beneficial. A third option is requesting that the resistant partner complete an intake testing package, which includes the Taylor-Johnson Temperament Analysis, a test in which the taker describes himself or herself as well as the partner. At first, the resistant spouse may only take the portion dealing with perceptions of the partner, but then the resistant spouse becomes curious. Once he or she comes in to discuss those perceptions, the spouse often continues with therapy.

Over the years I have found it helpful to explain several features during the initial session. First, I would like the couple's growth to move as rapidly as possible, and that is why I tend to take an active role in counseling as well as require homework. Second, I explain that, despite their probable hopes for immediate change and growth, we are all slow in giving up habit patterns, even ineffective ones. Though the change and growth will probably take longer than they anticipated, developing a new criterion for measuring success will encourage them that progress is occurring. That is, focusing upon the gains and changes rather than what remains the same will provide hope. A 3-percent improvement per week is rapid change. When a couple adopts this new criterion, obstacles that at one point seemed insurmountable can be overcome. Third, I explain that during the process of growth and stabilization new areas of conflict and hurt are often discovered. Instead of their viewing this as a setback or regression, they should see it as a sign of improvement. The patient (the marriage) is once again undergoing some major corrective surgery as part of the healing process. This up-front explanation has helped a number of couples when they hit rough spots in their counseling.

The subgoals of counseling will vary depending upon the couple. I often have these in advance—as described by the couple in the Marital Assessment Inventory (see p. 210). Sometimes, to clarify where we are going, I ask, "When our counseling is completed, how do you want yourself, your partner, and your marriage to be different?" If their response lacks clarity and their focus is only upon an immediate flare-up, it helps to have them reflect upon the question during the week and bring back a response in writing to the next session.

Our goal is not just solving the couple's presenting problem but discovering and eliminating the cause, teaching them skills so they do not need our assistance, and helping them develop an ongoing program of personal marital enrichment and a sense of hope for their marriage.

The spiritual life of the individual and the couple is both part of the healing process and a major developmental goal of counseling. As early as possible, the level of spiritual intimacy between the couple should be addressed because as it is discussed and nurtured, it can help bring other issues into focus. It has a soothing, stabilizing effect.

Perhaps one of the major ideals or beliefs that I want couples to grasp during the sessions is to move from an attitude of defeat to hope. I also want them to understand their call in marriage as a call to live out the truths of Scripture so that their marriage relationship reflects the active presence of Jesus Christ. My role is to encourage them by believing in their capability to grow.

Question 2
For what kind of people is your approach most appropriate?

The model I am proposing is suited to both professional counselors and those in local church ministry. But time constraints as well as the training level of pastors limit them to using just some of the suggested techniques and approaches.

The majority of clients I have seen over the years have been Christian, and yet there is no reason for my approach not to be effective with those who do not have the same belief structure. When the clients discover they are not being preached at, judged, or forced to consider the Christian perspective, they are eventually open to considering our value system. This is very likely when they begin to experience improvement in their relationship and become curious as to the origin of what is being shared with them in the sessions. If the question arises as to where these ideas are coming from, a statement such as the following is effective: "Many of the suggestions I've shared with you are not original. If you would ever like to consider more of them or look at them firsthand, let me know." This presents the opportunity to share with them for their own perusal either Scripture or the book I have used.

There have been times when I have said to clients, "I can offer you two types of suggestions. One will include recommendations and approaches to improve your marriage, but these have nothing to do with the spiritual dimension. The other is the same but with the addition of the spiritual resources to help you develop spiritual ⇒ intimacy in your marriage. Naturally, I have my own bias, but you need to be the ones who select which is most comfortable for you." I have not found counselees to be offended because of our differing belief systems if we exhibit a respect and acceptance of who and where they are in their lives.

My counseling format has been and is currently being used in premarital and marital counseling as well as in marriage-enrichment seminars. Because I have a strong educational background and have taught in graduate school for twenty-five years, my counseling has an educational foundation and flavor, which often is evident. And I find that what I say or teach can be expressed in a setting with one, two, or eighty individuals. There is a broad applicability. I do not believe that this model can only be effective for me. It can also be effective for others who learn the same principles and approach.

Question 3
What are your foci for counseling?

The significance of the person conducting the marital counseling cannot be overstated. A counselor is (hopefully) an objective catalyst who is there to provide insight, guidance, hope, and encouragement and to discover and nurture the abilities of husband and wife. For a multitude of reasons, we will not always succeed. But since our role is paramount, we must constantly study and learn. Furthermore, we must be aware of whom we work with best and whom we do not, conscious of our own unresolved personal and marital issues, and aware of both what we are saying and doing in counseling with any couple and why. Finally, we must be a reservoir of information, new insights, and resources to offer to any couple.

Over the past twenty years, I have become convinced that as therapists we need to model for the counselees what we are teaching or suggesting to them and to be so flexible that we can adapt to their thinking and communication style. This is the crux of establishing rapport quickly and moving ahead rapidly. To accomplish this, we must learn to expand and stretch and flex in our abilities. This means we need to understand our own culture, generational bias, personality preferences, gender inclinations, and thinking and communication styles. Then, based upon the knowledge of who we are and who the counselees are, we must adapt to speak their language.

A sixty-year old therapist can understand and relate to a young couple just as a woman therapist can understand and relate to a man. It takes study and work, but it is foundational. The following resources will be the most helpful to develop this expertise: *Counseling the Culturally Different* (Sue and Sue 1990), *Type Talk* (Krueger and Thuessen 1988), *Birth Order Roles and Sibling Patterns in Individual and Family Therapy* (Hoopes and Harper 1987), *How to Change Your Spouse Without Ruining Your Marriage* (Oliver and Wright 1992, esp. chaps. 4–5), *Counseling Baby Boomers* (Collins and Clinton), and *The People Puzzle* (Massey 1979).

Whether I begin the counseling by focusing on behavior, feelings, or cognition depends on the clients. If I approach feeling-oriented counselees on a cognitive level, we will not connect. However, shifting the approach so as to relate to who they are is very effective. As I connect with their orientation, it is then possible to assist and teach them to expand their abilities to relate better to their spouse's uniqueness, which is frequently the opposite of theirs.

To foster change in a marriage, I initially stress behavioral change reinforced by cognitive activity. To do this, I use numerous examples, illustrations, and structural homework assignments. But whatever we want to get across has to be packaged in such a way that each partner can understand it. To negate the packaging aspect or to de-emphasize any one of the three areas (behavior, cognition, feelings) can hinder lasting change in the life of the individual as well as in his or her relationship.

I believe that distorted thinking and perceptions both create and perpetuate marital discord. Eventually, a refinement or correction of thought-life can lead to stability.

Question 4
How is your marriage counseling conducted?

The counseling process actually begins prior to the initial session because the couple (or one partner) is asked to complete the Marital Assessment Inventory (MAI; see Additional Resources on p. 210).

This very detailed, eleven-page inventory helps the client express information concerning his or her family structure and background, marriage preparation, personal family background, personal information, and evaluation of the marriage. The marital evaluation includes tasks and qualities that the person appreciates about his or her partner and requests and expectations that each has for the other. In addition, the client ranks and evaluates twenty-four specific areas of the marriage, with the couple's spiritual relationship, finances, decision making, and family issues evaluated in greatest detail. The final page, which assists the counselor in selecting a direction for the first session, draws out the individual's goals and level of hopefulness for counseling, the amount of time per week the client can give to the marriage, the level of change the client is willing to make for the marriage to succeed, the individual's commitment to staying in the marriage, and the perceived commitment level of the partner. The last two items can very well indictate the direction to be taken in the initial session. If one partner is leaning out of the marriage and the other leaning in, the counselor may need to ask the latter to give more initially. This is necessary in order to encourage the former to stay in counseling as well as to have a sense of hope that the partner will change.

When clients complete the inventory prior to counseling, the initial session does not have to be used for history taking or basic-information gathering. Couples respond very well to the explanation that completing these forms can save several hours of counseling time; thus, we can proceed much faster. Another benefit of the written inventory is that each partner has had the opportunity to do a thorough evaluation of the marriage. Since most tend to over-emphasize negatives, questions that elicit positive responses can assist in creating a more balanced perspective of the relationship. And this is part of my goal in the initial session—discovering strengths and positives rather than just problems and pain. In so doing, I am better able to generate hope and positive expectancies for counseling and for their marriage.

I would like to see progress occur as rapidly as possible, but it is difficult to give a couple an exact time of how long counseling will take. Some couples will say that they will come for just a set number of sessions. If so, it is important to determine how they want to be different at the conclusion.

I favor a fairly active approach with couples, but not to the extent of being overbearing or overriding their personalities. A therapist's activity demonstrates that the therapist is interested in seeing something occur within the couple's marriage and life. A passive aloofness does not register well with most couples. Too often I have heard couples complain that when they sought a marriage counselor, the therapist just sat there and listened but did not help. Couples want help and guidance because they probably have a feeling of desperation. Even with an active approach, the couple can still discover new approaches and solutions.

I rely heavily upon outside homework in the form of interactive activities, books, and audiotapes. The time in counseling is best spent reinforcing, amplifying, and applying what the couple discovered in the outside work, which in turn accelerates the progress of counseling. Whatever is used for homework must be applicable to current counseling issues. When it is, progress is accelerated. Over the years, I have been amazed at the effectiveness of some outside resources, such as the "Love Life" tapes by Ed Wheat. I have seen numerous couples make a sudden and radical change of direction in their relationship after listening several times to this series and applying it to their lives. That, coupled with my assisting them in developing the spiritual dimension of their marriage, has brought about significant growth.

There are times when I wonder if I have provided sufficient guidance or too much guidance. With each couple, it is a learning process to discover how much interchange is necessary to gain an understanding of their interactive process as well as to let them express themselves sufficiently in order to feel they have been heard. Of necessity, each session varies because I do not want the sessions or myself to be predictable. As I review a session on tape, I might hear directive couple interaction, spontaneous interaction, or a discussion between myself and one partner for a period of time. And yet another session is totally different because the criterion for what occurs is based upon the moment's pressing need. I use a tentative tone and wording in my questions and statements to keep from putting unnecessary pressure on the partners to comply.

Question 5
How do you deal with a few of the common marital problems?

A frequent issue between couples is unmet needs. A simple approach described by several therapists is the observance of caring days or cherishing days. Each partner lists twelve to fifteen loving or caring behaviors he or she would like the other to do. When a partner receives the other's list, he or she has a road map or a guide to follow for his or her endeavors. Each partner selects one or two behaviors to give each day. This approach takes a willingness and commitment on the part of each person to follow through regardless of what the other does. If the approach is followed, in time, these positive behaviors become a part of the couple's regular interaction.

When it comes to extramarital involvement—if one spouse is currently involved in an affair and both spouses come for counseling—the third party must be expelled from the marriage. It is difficult for the noninvolved spouse and the therapist to compete with this third party. *Broken Promises* by Henry Virkler (1992) is the most helpful volume in print on this subject.

I am not sure how original the following interventions are, but I use them frequently in the cases of individuals or couples considering divorce. I want him, her, or them to be fully cognizant of the ramifications of this step (which many are not). I do not immediately attempt to talk them out of divorce because often they are, or one is, already in a defensive stance, and my attempt could intensify this. However, I ask if they believe they have taken every step possible to build their marriage, if they believe they have given it 150-percent effort. If not, I suggest that we commit to three months of counseling. If at the end of that time there has been no improvement, at least they can say they really did put forth sufficient effort. I request the following for the three-month period: (a) neither should mention or threaten divorce to the spouse; (b) they each should listen to the "Love Life" tapes and read *Divorce Busting* by Michele Weiner-Davis; and (c) they should attend (if possible) a divorce-recovery workshop or meeting to simply listen to the stories of those going through the process. Heightening their awareness of the divorce process will hopefully cause them to reconsider this option and move toward marriage. Such awareness may generate some discomfort, but who ever said counseling would be comfortable and painless?

If a divorce has occurred or is in process, I will work with whoever comes to me to assist them in recovering. If a divorced individual is coming for premarital counseling, I will not begin until sufficient time has elapsed since the divorce for stabilization and until they have completed a divorce-recovery program.

Another approach I take with couples is to ask the question, "If what you are doing isn't working, why keep doing it? There's got to be a better way. What have you got to lose by trying it?" For the greatest impact, the question must be adapted to the counselee's life and frame of reference. I was told by a physician's wife that this very question was what caused her husband to turn from forty years of negative responses to consider a positive approach. Frankly, I did not remember what I had said to him until she reminded me, but I framed the question in this way, "If you operated on fifteen patients who all had the same disorder and they all died, you'd consider changing your procedure, wouldn't you?" He saw the light. I think it is possible to make just about any statement to a person or to confront a person if we use the proper tone of voice and exhibit care and concern.

Another approach I use helps a couple relinquish their defensiveness toward each other and develop a willingness to consider the other perspective. On the MAI, there is a section where each is to write down the requests he or she has for the spouse at the present time. Usually, the spouse is aware of these requests, hears about them frequently, and resists them. I go over the requests with both spouses and discuss their perspectives on and responses to them. We then enter a new process that I call My Spouse Is Right. I say, "Let's assume that your partner's requests (and/or complaints) are accurate. If so, what would it take for you to comply? What steps would you take? What could your partner do to assist you in changing? What might it cost you to take this step?" Because we are speculating and talking "as if," the resistance is lessened, and the partners discover that taking these various stances could help marital growth.

Yet another approach I use involves a somewhat different application of the Taylor-Johnson Temperament Analysis. Both partners take the test as they see themselves and also as each sees the other. To facilitate communication and resolution of conflictual issues between the partners, we discuss the individual questions that are used to construct each trait, focusing especially on the expressive/inhibited, sympathetic/indifferent, and hostile/tolerant traits. By comparing how each person perceived himself or herself with how he or she was perceived by the other, we have ample material to discuss. I then ask the two to sit face-to-face and discuss their responses. If one interrupts to defend his or her position, I move in with further structure so each can learn to hear and consider the partner's perspective.

Past accumulated hurts lead to resentment. This is a major blockage in marriage. Regardless of the offense, whether large or small, in time the hurt and the anger build. Whether working with just one or with both partners, I can use the same approach. Especially here, written or taped homework assignments can be beneficial. First, each person is instructed to write down the hurts and how each hurt affected him or her. Each is also instructed to write an angry letter to the partner and to sit in a room alone and read the letter to an empty chair, which represents the partner. These first two steps serve to drain the emotional intensity. The next step is for each to write a letter of forgiveness as well as a vision of what he or she would like the marriage to become. Each is encouraged to read this letter to an empty chair as well. Often all or some of these letters are shared in the counseling session. A spouse who has created the greatest hurt or broken the marriage vow needs to know that his or her partner's journey of forgiveness will take time. It is gradual and cannot be rushed. Usually, the offended partner will want to bring up and discuss issues more than the other. Two exceptionally helpful books in this area are *Torn Asunder* by Dave Carder (1992) and *When the Vow Breaks* by Joseph Warren Kniskern (1993).

Task 1
Respond to the case study by telling precisely how you might typically treat it, in how many sessions, in what order, and with what responses by the clients throughout counseling. One restriction: Assume that between the third and fourth counseling sessions with you—regardless of what had gone on during the previous session—the couple had a major argument and come to the fourth session in some crisis.

As Art and Pam enter into therapy, hopefully they will have had the opportunity to complete the MAI prior to the initial session. Information from the inventory would then serve as a platform from which to launch an intervention.

In the initial session, I would like Art and Pam to share a five-to-ten-minute summation of his own and her own perspective of the main difficulties. It would be additionally helpful to hear what each believes he or she has contributed to the situation, what each believes the spouse feels is the problem, and finally specifically how each wants the marriage to be different when the counseling is over. Following each spouse's presentation, I might add to it any information contained in the MAI that he or she did not mention verbally. This helps to elicit additional information from each as well as to let both of them know that the therapist has taken the time to assess their relationship.

After the summations and my additions to them from the MAI, there are numerous ways to proceed. Since most couples are vague and fuzzy on goal setting (what they actually want to be different), it is often helpful to spend time clarifying these issues so as to provide a greater sense of direction. Another possibility is to use the section from the MAI that asked what each appreciates about the other and then spend time creating a list of eight to ten strengths each sees in the other. Often the strengths are there but tend to be overlooked and neglected. Either approach, setting goals or recognizing strengths, can provide a sense of hope and encouragement for the couple and keeps them from dominating the initial session with a litany of complaints or faultfindings.

As the sessions with Art and Pam continue, there are numerous subject areas to explore. I will now identify these and describe my approach to them.

Future Focus

Although it is helpful for each partner to understand his or her own contribution to each of the negative issues, it is vital in every discussion to turn each partner's thinking toward the future and the possibilities. Often I use the question, "What will you be doing this week that will make a difference in a positive way?"

Emotional Intimacy

Since there is a loss of emotional intimacy and Art and Pam's feelings are "almost extinguished," it would be helpful to explore what it was like when there was emotional intimacy. I would begin by asking any kind of question to better understand what they had. Who did what? How did each feel? When and where did it occur? What did intimacy mean to each? Given the male gender difference, Art's home environment, and his own cognitive bent, I question whether he could even access his feelings let alone connect on an emotional level. Perhaps what they thought they had was superficial. In any case, a further question to explore is, "What will it take now from each of you, independent of what the other does, to build an even better level of intimacy in your marriage?"

Another possible way to provide hope for the rebuilding of intimacy is to use the courtship analysis. There are two reasons for reviewing the courtship. First, couples need to remember the intense feelings of love for each other. Many couples begin counseling asking why they married each other in the first place and whether they ever really loved each other. By reviewing their courtship, you can help establish hope for what can occur in the marriage now. Couples who were quite romantic during courtship may now feel led to exert more effort to commit themselves to redevelop their relationship. Second, the couple needs to rediscover what each other had intended to do in terms of responsibilities and behavior and what each other had intended to give. Questions to use in this endeavor follow.

When did you last touch each other affectionately?

What did you think of the other when you first kissed?

What attracted you to each other?

What was your courtship like?

How did you meet?

Where did you meet?

What were the circumstances of your meeting?

Infertility

Numerous problems occur in individuals and in marriages because people fail to completely grieve over a loss. I would thus explore with Art and Pam how each dealt with Art's functional sterility. During one of the sessions, it may be beneficial for Art and Pam to sit face-to-face in a safe atmosphere (the therapist's office) and share their feelings with each other.

Infidelity

Art and Pam both said Art's affair has been forgiven and forgotten. What does that mean? What were the exact circumstances that led to the affair? How did each contribute to the circumstances? Have Pam's anger and hurt and Art's guilt been fully resolved? What does Pam need from Art in order to trust him at this time? The infidelity appears to be an unresolved issue for the couple. Lewis Smedes's book *Forgive and Forget* would be useful here.

Family of Origin

Family-of-origin issues involve expectations partners have for their marriage because of their own family, their level of comfort in relating to each other's family, and feelings about the level of family involvement and about adjustments to be made to the level. I would perhaps discuss with Art and Pam ways to confront the in-law issues directly.

Personality Differences

At some time after Art and Pam's marriage has shown improvement and growth, I would use the Myers-Briggs Type Indicator with them, in session and through outside reading, to clarify their personality differences. Upon recognizing the differences, each can be led to approaching the other differently so there is a better response. In addition, such recognition can move them closer to functioning in a complementary fashion.

Relationship Roles

In Art and Pam's marriage, the relationship-dynamics issues are significant. To address them, there are a couple of ways to proceed. One approach is to have them contract to spend together each day a negotiated amount of time. A second is to ask them to reverse roles (i.e., the pursuer becomes the distancer, and vice versa) during a session, and perhaps even for a week. The role reversal may bring a new meaning to both.

To further address the dynamics of Art and Pam's relationship, I would ask each to take part in the other's recreational activities once a week for a limited period of time. Through the activity, they may discover that it is possible for them to relate to each other. It might also be helpful for them to explore and discover a new source of recreation that each could enjoy.

Communication Styles

During the counseling sessions and at home, it may be helpful for Art and Pam to have a tape recorder on hand so that each can develop more insight into his or her communication style and patterns of interruption. Since interruption denotes a lack of listening, teaching both partners listening-reflecting techniques to use during the week is necessary. I would ask them during the session to engage in an argument, which I would record and play back to make them conscious of their interruptive patterns so that these will eventually be eliminated.

I would also use the discussion in the session as well as assigned reading for Art to clarify his anger. Each partner should understand the three major causes of anger—fear, hurt, and frustration. Once these are understood, then the core issues, rather than the symptoms, can become the focus, helping to diminish both the defensiveness and the anger.

The Blame Game

When Art and Pam engage in blaming, it would be helpful to have them evaluate what blaming accomplishes and whether or not their partner ever accepts the blame. I would then ask them to reframe their statements of blame so that the sentences are less emotionally charged. I would further ask, "If you didn't have your partner to blame for this situation, who would you then say is the responsible party?" Art and Pam might then recognize their own contributions.

Crisis Response

When any couple comes in reporting the occurrence of a major crisis during the week, some sort of damage assessment is necessary. If the partners are really in a crisis state, their main objectives are to sustain the marriage, stabilize the feelings, and reestablish some sort of equilibrium into their lives and relationship. Only when these goals are met can we actually work through the problem.

If Art and Pam had experienced a midweek crisis, I would ask each one to describe what happened, how it affected him or her, how it emotionally affected the other, and how much of a setback it was for the growth of the relationship. I might also ask them to reenact a portion of the argument. As they proceed, I might intervene with suggestions, helping them discover what they would have preferred saying and doing. I would also work with them to set up written guidelines for conduct during arguments. For the guidelines to be effective, each must sign the agreement and review it several times a day.

Both Pam and Art have said they pray about their marriage and want it to work out. Thus, in the session we would need to spend a significant amount of time clarifying how they pray and what they pray for and teaching them a new level of spiritual intimacy.

Task 2
Create a dialogue between the counselor and the couple (or one spouse, if you prefer) showing how you might deal with communication difficulties.

Counselor:	I am interested in hearing about your week, especially the times when you were problem solving.
Art:	We did a lot of talking, but I'm not too sure I saw any problems solved. It was more like a rehash of what went on before.
Counselor:	So, from your perspective, you talked about issues you previously discussed. What was different about it this time?
Art:	I guess the only thing that was different was it didn't go on forever and, well, I wasn't as angry.
Counselor:	So you're saying it might have been better in a small way?
Art:	Yeah, very small. But I guess any progress is better than none at all.
Counselor:	That it is. Before you came today were you conscious that it was a step in the right direction?

Art: [*pause*] I guess not. You're probably suggesting that I ought to keep my eyes open and notice the small steps of progress, right?

Counselor: I can see you've been listening. That's progress. I have a question for you. When I ask Pam how she felt about this past week, what might she say was better for her?

Art: I'm not really sure . . .

Counselor: What would you hope she would say?

Art: I think I would like her to say—

Counselor: [*interrupting*] Would you turn to Pam and talk with her in the first person?

Art: Pam, I, uh, I think I would hope to hear you say, if not today, then sometime in the future, that during the past week I listened to you a little better and didn't interrupt you as much. I, if I don't get as angry, hope that you would notice any improvement no matter how small it is and let me know about it. I need to hear from you that you notice my efforts and that it means something to you. It's hard to make changes anyway and worse when they go unrecognized. I'm trying to stay in the discussions with you, and the half-hour time limit gives me some hope that we won't be talking all night, but pressuring me to talk doesn't work—

Counselor: You changed directions.

Art: What do you mean?

Counselor: You changed from sharing what you thought or hoped she would say to lecturing and blaming, and your tone of voice started to become intense. This is a pattern that's happened for years, isn't it?

Art: I don't think I did that.

Counselor: Let me back up the tape on the recorder and listen to what you shared. [*The counselor rewinds the tape so Art can hear what he said and how he said it.*]

	Art, what's your response to what you heard?
Art:	[*pause*] Tape recorders don't lie, do they? I guess I did shift into blaming, and my tone became more definite, more intense, more . . .
Counselor:	More angry?
Art:	Yes, more angry.
Counselor:	In the future as you become more aware of your tendency, what will you do when you catch yourself blaming or becoming angry?
Art:	I think I will—
Counselor:	Would you turn and tell Pam directly?
Art:	This is different. [*pause*] Pam, what I want to say to you is, uh, I want to be different, but it's not that easy. In the future, if or when I start to blame or get angry and if I recognize it, I will say, "That's not what I wanted to say, and this is what I want to say." Yeah, I like that. I think I could do that if I'm aware that I'm being a jerk again.
Counselor:	I hear your wanting to be aware, but you're not too sure you can recognize it. Do you need Pam to give you some assistance?
Art:	That might be helpful, even though I'd rather be able to do it myself, but I don't have the confidence that I can.
Counselor:	What could Pam say in the meantime to help you until you develop the ability to interrupt your old negative patterns? What can she say or do that you won't take offense to and become even more upset?
Art:	Hmmm. That's a good point. I guess you're saying I have to give her permission to say something along with the assurance I'm not going to get ticked off at her for doing it. Right?
Counselor:	You're right. It's up to you to decide, give her some guidance, and then not bite her head off when she does.
Art:	That will be new. OK, here goes. Pam, when you

hear me either blaming you or getting angry, maybe you could say either "blame" or "anger" and that would help me recognize what I'm doing so I could correct it.

Counselor: That's an excellent suggestion. And what can she expect from you in terms of assurance when she does this?

Art: I think she can—

Counselor: [*interrupting*] Tell Pam.

Art: I will accept what you say. I might stop talking for a while to regroup and get my emotions under control, and then I'll respond. But don't assume that I'm going to withdraw because I won't. I agree to that.

Counselor: Pam, we've dominated the time so far talking with Art and talking with you some of the time. Before you and I talk, is it all right for me to ask him one more question about you?

Pam: Yes, certainly. And I guess I'm curious about what it is.

Counselor: Art, how do you think Pam might be feeling right now after this interchange? Not what she thinks, but how she feels.

Art: You're still after me to get into that feeling stuff, aren't you?

Counselor: Yes, especially if you want to speak her language and for the two of you to be on the same level.

Art: I guess Pam may be feeling that, uh, there may be some hope for our relationship. Hopeful, yeah, that might be the word. I don't think she's joyful or elated, but maybe encouraged. How are those words?

Counselor: Excellent. You're able to do it. You're open to learning. The next step is sharing how you feel, but we'll deal with that later. Pam, how do you feel about what you've heard so far?

Pam: I had mixed feelings about the past week, but I wasn't as negative about it as Art. The fact that he didn't withdraw even when my mouth started working overtime again was encouraging. And then to hear for the first time a definite plan and a commitment to doing something different does encourage me. Honestly I do wonder what will happen when I say the words "blame" or "anger." I hope it works. I want it to work. But I am apprehensive.

Counselor: What will you do if there is a negative response to your calling Art back to his commitment? Will you tell him right now?

Pam: Art, first of all, I believe that you want to be different and speak differently. You can do it. If there's a relapse, I will just repeat what I said before. No, I'll do more than that. I'll write them on cards and hold them up so you can read them. Our therapist has said you respond best to seeing things, so I'll do that. And when you do anything positive, I'll notice it and let you know. I need the same from you.

Counselor: So you're willing to respond in a positive way even if there is a relapse? Both of you seem to have the desire to make your relationship different. And you both want your efforts to be recognized by the other.

References

Ables, B. 1977. *Couples in therapy.* San Francisco: Jossey-Bass.

Carder, D. 1992. *Torn asunder.* Chicago: Moody.

Collins, G., and T. Clinton. *Counseling baby boomers.* Waco, Tex.: Word Books.

Hoopes, M., and J. M. Harper. 1987. *Birth order roles and sibling patterns in individual and family therapy.* Rockville, Md.: Aspen.

Kniskern, J. W. 1993. *When the vow breaks.* Nashville: Broadman.

Krueger, O., and J. M. Thuessen. 1988. *Type talk.* Garden City, N.Y.: Tilden Press, Doubleday.

Massey, M. E. 1979. *The people puzzle.* Reston, Va.: Reston Publishing Company.

Oliver, G. J., and H. N. Wright. 1992. *When anger hits home.* Chicago: Moody.

———. 1994. *How to change your spouse without ruining your marriage.* Ann Arbor: Servant.

Richmond, G. 1988. *The divorce decision.* Waco, Tex.: Word Books.

Smedes, L. B. 1984. *Forgive and forget.* San Francisco: Harper and Row.

Stuart, R. B. 1980. *Helping couples change.* New York: Guilford.

Sue, D. W., and D. Sue. 1990. *Counseling the culturally different.* New York: Wiley.

Wheat, E. *Love life.* Audiotapes.

Wilcoxon, A., and D. Fenell. 1983. Engaging the nonattending spouse in marital therapy through the use of therapist-initiated communication. *Journal of Marital and Family Therapy* 9:199–203.

Virkler, H. 1992. *Broken promises.* Dallas: Word Books.

Weiner-Davis, M. 1992. *Divorce busting.* New York: Summit Books.

Wile, D. B. 1981. *Couples therapy.* New York: Wiley.

Wright, H. N. 1986. *Self-talk, imagery, and prayer in counseling.* Waco, Tex.: Word Books.

———. 1990. *Quiet times for couples.* Eugene, Ore.: Harvest House.

———. 1991a. *Holding onto romance.* Ventura, Calif.: Regal Books.

———. 1991b. *Recovering from the losses of life.* Grand Rapids: Baker.

———. 1992. *Premarital counseling handbook.* Chicago: Moody.

———. 1993. *Crisis counseling.* Ventura, Calif.: Regal Books.

———. 1995. *Secrets of a lasting marriage.* Ventura, Calif.: Regal Books.

Additional Resources

The Marital Assessment Inventory can be purchased through Christian Marriage Enrichment, 17821 17th Street, #190, Tustin, California 92680.

Exploring Christian Marriage Counseling

Jennifer S. Ripley and
Everett L. Worthington Jr.

D eveloping a theory of Christian marital counseling is like running a maze. Theories begin with a common goal—improving marriages. However, each theorist winds along a different path from the beginning of therapy to its end. As different as the eight chapters in this book are, all eight have provided models of Christian marital counseling that have influenced therapists and trainees throughout the country. How have they influenced you? How do their theories of marital counseling affect your couples therapy? How do or will you conduct your sessions when couples seek your help in their marriage?

In this chapter, we provide a mental map of various paths through the maze of marital counseling to help you find, or continue to define, your own path. We review each counselor's theory and style of interaction. We tackle some key questions for Christian marital counseling and discuss our theorists' answers to these questions. When we're done, we hope you understand some fundamental choices that Christian marital counselors must make.

Question 1
What are the basics of your theory of marriage counseling? In your description, include your view of the typical cause(s) of marital problems and the typical goals of counseling.

In answering Question 1, Christian marital theorists addressed three issues: Christian concepts, psychological concepts, and concepts of integration.

Christian Concepts

What is *Christian* about Christian marital counseling? Several Christian themes are found within the eight theories of marital counseling.

Guernsey, Joy, and Oliver and Miller incorporate the *imago dei*—persons created in the image of God—into their theories. To them, people and their well-being are significant; therefore, counseling is important in God's eyes.

Guernsey, Harley, and Worthington bring out the resemblance between God's covenants with his people (e.g., Mosaic, Davidic, new) and the partners' marriage covenants with each other. For these theories, marriages are not contractual, wherein one partner gives of himself or herself only if the other partner does as well. For them, marriages are covenantal, wherein partners give of themselves regardless of the response of their spouse. This theme illustrates a common belief among Christians that marriage is designed or ordained by God, giving it a position of prominence in society and among interpersonal relationships. The theme of the covenant helps to give weight and purpose to the work in which Christian marital counselors engage.

Another Christian theme is the similarity of the dynamics of marital love and of God's love for the Son and for the church (Joy, Worthington). Two theorists suggest that promoting marital love is the most important goal of marital therapy (Harley, Worthington).

The most common Christian-derived theme among the theorists is the belief that marriages suffer because partners are sinful (Guernsey; Harley; Joy; Oliver and Miller; Stanley, Trathen, and McCain; Worthington; Wright). Marital counseling generally aims at helping couples overcome sin in their relationship.

Psychological Concepts

What approaches from the field of secular psychology do Christian marital counselors employ? As might be expected, counselors' theories differ substantially.

Systems. Wright, the Parrotts, and Oliver and Miller claim to rely on a systems model of therapy. However, these Christian marital counselors seem to use "systems" to denote merely that married partners intimately influence each other so intricately that they must be addressed together for change to occur. The "systems" label is, therefore, loosely applied.

The Parrotts are most clearly identified with a discrete systems theory—that of Bowen. Still there is little evidence that any of the counselors in this book would endorse modern systems concepts, such as circular causality, or radical-constructionist views. Oliver and Miller, with the Couples Communication program (formerly the Minnesota Couples Communication Program), propose that they are grounded in systems theory. However, behavioral marital therapy, which focuses on conversation exchanges and skill building, is evidenced in many aspects of their theory. In addition, they promote self-awareness of sense data, thoughts, feelings, and wants, which suggests abiding influences of Carl Rogers and, perhaps, psychodynamic ideas. Clearly, Oliver and Miller have integrated several theories in their approach. Wright gives even less attention to systems theory than do the Parrotts and Oliver and Miller.

Psychodynamic. Advocating a psychodynamic model, Guernsey and the Parrotts focus on the patterns present in families of origin and believe that a couple's experiences with those families are integrated into the couple's marriage. Although Guernsey evidences psychodynamic influences, he also incorporates behavioral techniques in his practice, as manifest in the marriage conference he proposed for Art and Pam (see pp. 36–37). Similarly, the Parrotts integrate cognitive-behavioral traditions with their Bowenian influences, especially when they focus on marriage myths. (Bowen's roots are in evolutionary and psychodynamic theories.)

Cognitive-social learning theory. Stanley, Trathen, and McCain are most clearly identified with cognitive-social learning marital therapy. Their goal is to change the thinking and behavior of the couple, which helps lead to prevention or solution of marital difficulties. According to their view, if a couple can learn positive cognition and behavior, then their marriage is capable of blooming into beauty.

Integration of psychological theories. Wright (1981) and Worthington (1989) have relied heavily in the past on cognitive-behavioral theories. Although their current writings are more eclectic than previous ones, the early influence of cognitive-behavior therapy is clear in their essentially cognitive dialogues with couples and their concern for the couples' expectations about marriage. At present, Wright and Worthington both draw from solution-oriented therapy (deShazer 1988), which advocates a limited focus in therapy, a short-term model, and specific goal setting to reach a solution to a couple's problem. Their approaches reflect a trend in therapy toward a convergence of theories, a trend spurred by the secular integration-of-psychotherapies movement.[1]

Generally, today few therapists use a single orientation to therapy; indeed, most are eclectic, integrative, or transtheoretical. No longer can a novice therapist simply choose a theory of counseling and follow its rules. Pressures demand critical evaluation of theories, techniques, and analyses of philosophical and practical consistencies and inconsistencies. The formulation of a personal approach to marital

1. The main proponents of the integration-of-psychotherapies movement are Norcross (1993) and others (Beitman, Goldfried, and Norcross 1989) who often publish in the Journal for Psychotherapy Integration. Pressures by managed mental-health care companies toward briefer, more solution-focused therapies also influence integration principles.

counseling is no small task, as it will define the goals, course, and outcome of marital therapy, which will become increasingly evident.

Integrating Christian and Secular Concepts

Upon surveying the theories of Christian marital counselors, we recognize clearly that no single Christian approach nor secular theory has influenced all therapists. Moreover, how Christian therapists integrate Christian and psychological ideas suggests variety and, perhaps, controversy. Three general approaches to integrating Christian ideas with secular theories are evident: Christian ideas (a) are thoroughly incorporated into most aspects of the theory, (b) serve as underlying assumptions of counseling theory, and (c) are somewhat dissociated from the theory and practice.

Incorporated into theory. Some theorists incorporate Christian ideas into almost every aspect of their theory. For example, Worthington weaves the concept of "faith working through love" throughout his theory, and his goal of discipleship in counseling is directly dependent on Christian concepts. His approach thus provides clients with a biblically based "story" through which they can understand counseling. While most of Worthington's counseling methods are derived from secular theories, they are conceptualized within the framework of promoting faith, work, and love, to which he refers repeatedly.

Underlie the theory. Other theorists (e.g., Harley; Oliver and Miller) use Christian themes as underlying assumptions of counseling but employ secular psychological theory in counseling sessions, for they believe that Christian concepts directly apply to some areas of counseling but not to others. An analogy would be physicians who believe that some activities (e.g., surgery) need not have a Christian conceptualization, while other aspects of medicine do (e.g., bedside manner or healing the sick). Oliver and Miller and Harley have Christian presuppositions (e.g., it is God's will for couples to stay married and meet each other's needs), but their theories appear more grounded in psychology than in the Bible or explicit Christian thinking. Oliver and Miller explain that their theory is consistent with God's plan for marriages: God desires people to communicate well. They also emphasize that people's sinful nature causes problems in communication. While these theorists integrate Christian ideas into the presuppositions of their theory, little of the explicit theory or practice refers to Christian concepts.

Dissociated from theory. Guernsey's approach has a theological core, yet his counseling seems to run on a different track than does his theology. Indeed, his theology is not directly worked into his counseling theory. He states that what makes his counseling Christian is that Christians participate in it. Many Christian counselors and therapists will resonate with Guernsey's approach, which is consistent with psychodynamic theory that strives to minimize the intrusion of a therapist's values in any kind of therapy, including marital therapy.

Diversity in approaches. The numerous ways to integrate Christian concepts and secular theories into Christian marital counseling illustrate how truly diverse the field is. There are no agreed-upon standards for integrating Christian and psychological beliefs. Are one's Christian beliefs the cause and reason to do counseling? Do the counselor's Christian beliefs make counseling Christian? Does the structure of Christian counseling rest on biblical analogies or the use during counseling of ecclesiastical practices such as prayer or forgiveness, and if so, how much? Some counselors (none in the present volume) believe that counseling should rely *wholly* on biblical concepts, without referring to secular psychology at all. Others primarily use secular psychological constructs and practices. There are several distinct camps in the controversy, but no bloodshed.

The integration of Scripture into counseling. Reviewing the authors' use of references and concepts from Scripture provides some insight into their integration practices (see table 1). Most therapists included some biblical reference or concept in answering the question on the basics of his or her theory of marital counseling. Although the authors cited a wide variety of Old and New Testament references, they referred most frequently to the concepts from Genesis 1–3 that persons are created in the image of God and that in Adam and Eve humans fell from grace. Other common references include Ephesians 5, concerning the roles of husbands and wives (vv. 22–33), and passages emphasizing the importance of love and romance in marriage (e.g., Song of Songs; 1 Cor. 13).

Table 1

Scripture Integration of the Theorists:
Biblical References within
Theorists' Answers to Each Question

Theorist(s)	References and Concepts
Guernsey	Gen. 1:26–27[Q1]; 1:27[Q1]; Exod. 32[Q1]; 2 Sam. 11–12[Q1]; Matt. 19:6[Q1]; Mark 2:23–3:6[Q1]; John 16:7–11[Q1]; Rom. 3:23[Q1]; covenant[Q1]; evil[Q1]; sin[Q1]
Harley	Matt. 5–7[Q1]
Joy	Gen. chap. 1[Q5, T2]; 1:26[Q1]; 1:27[Q1]; chap. 2[T2]; 2:24[Q1]; chap. 3[Q5, T2]; Exod. 20[T2]; Hos. 2:16[Q5]
Oliver and Miller	Gen. 1:26[Q1]; chap. 3[Q1]; four Gospels[Q1]
Parrott and Parrott	Gen. 2:24[Q3, Q5]; forgiveness[T1]
Stanley, Trathen, and McCain	Gen. chap. 2[Q1]; 3:10[Q1]; Prov. 12:18[Q1]; 15:1[Q1]; 29:11[Q1]; Song of Songs[Q1]; Mal. 2:15–16[Q5]; Matt. 19:6[Q1]; 23:26[Q3]; 1 Cor. 13[Q1, Q4]; Gal. 5:13–15[Q1]; Eph. 4:25–27[Q1]; chap. 5[Q1]; 5:32[Q1]; James 1:19[T1]; 1 Peter 3:9–10[Q1]; 1 John 4:10–18[T1]; 4:18[T1]; Rev. 2:4–5[T1]; Adam and Eve[Q1]
Worthington	Prov. 27:17[Q1]; Matt. 6:33[Q1]; Gal. 5:6[Q1, T1]; Heb. 11:1[Q1]; Adam and Eve[T2]; forgiveness[Q5, T1]; Joshua[Q5, T1]
Wright	prayer[T1]; Scripture[Q2]

Superscript key: Q1 = Question 1; Q2 = Question 2; Q3 = Question 3; Q4 = Question 4; Q5 = Question 5; T1 = Task 1; T2 = Task 2

By reviewing table 1, we can see how heavily Scripture is integrated into these brief writings on theory and practice. On one hand, Oliver and Miller and Worthington used a high degree of Scripture integration in their theories but were more vague in their case-study practice. Guernsey relied heavily on Scripture for his theological core, but did not include it in his psychological theory. On the other hand, Joy referred to Scripture often in practice and theory.

We are not trying to draw broad conclusions about any of these theorists and their stance on Scripture itself. The sample of material is much too small to make meaningful comparisons, and we believe it would be inappropriate and likely inaccurate if anyone were to treat our generalizations as more than they are. They are simply a vehicle for illustrating the myriad of choices facing Christian marital therapists today.

Developing your style of integration. The preceding analysis of integration practices leads to the question, How much *should* Christian marital counselors actually integrate Scripture into therapy? Does the background of counselors who are trained in secular theories and within secular universities essentially prohibit heavy integration of Scripture into practice as compared to the background of counselors who are trained as pastors and within seminaries? Pastors and seminary-trained therapists might challenge secular-university-trained Christian marital counselors to more often employ the power of Scripture to help Christian marriages. However, some counselors might respond that most couples do not come to marital counseling for spiritual guidance but specifically for help with their marriage.

In counseling, what is the optimal balance of Christianity and psychology? Christian marital counselors face the serious task of deciding what balance is best for them, their clients, and their practice. Each strategy has solid reasoning behind it, and none seems to sway all Christian therapists. In most cases, one could predict a therapist's stance on integrating Christianity and psychology by knowing the psychological theory to which the therapist subscribes. For example, most counselors who are heavily influenced by psychoanalytic theory, which advises therapists to minimize disclosure of their own values to clients, tend to minimize the use of overt Christian language, practices, and techniques. Most therapists who are heavily influenced by cognitive theory, which advises therapists to directly address beliefs and values to promote therapeutic change, use Christian language and techniques overtly.

Our challenge to theorists is this: What is the source for therapists' worldviews? Where do we form our assumptions about the purpose of marriage and relationships and about the ways to help married partners? Do we begin from psychological theory or biblical theology, or some combination of the two? Do we begin with personal experience in our family of origin or in our own relationship history? Do we value research, theology, or experience? The therapist's starting point may indeed orient him or her toward his or her ending point.

Question 2
For what kind of people is your approach most appropriate?

Each marital therapist practices within a specific context. Some work as pastors, pastoral counselors, therapists in private practice, therapists in church-supported agencies, or therapists in explicitly Christian agencies. Some of these are dependent on insurance or managed-care companies for financial support. Regardless of employment context, the marital counselor's theory must be appropriate for the clientele of that context. Some approaches in the present book are suited for particular settings and clientele, while others are broadly applicable.

Remediation, Prevention, or Enrichment?

The main applications of marital theories can be divided into three aspects—remediation of problems (marital therapy), prevention of difficulties (premarital or neomarital counseling), and enrichment (the promotion of better marriages among already well-functioning marriages)—or into some combination of the three (see table 2).

Theorists who advocated more eclectic and integrated theories also suggested that their models are appropriate for several applications. Stanley, Trathen, and McCain; Wright; Worthington; and Oliver and Miller, for example, each work with couples in remediation, prevention, and enrichment. On the other hand, Guernsey and Harley use their more defined styles to work primarily with remediation, while Joy works mostly with enrichment. The Parrotts center on prevention and remediation during early marriage.

Table 2

Focus of Theory: Ratings of Applicability of Each Theory to Prevention, Remediation, and Enrichment

Theorist(s)	Prevention	Remediation	Enrichment
Guernsey	Low	High	Moderate
Harley	Moderate	High	Moderate
Joy	Low	Moderate	High
Oliver and Miller	High	Moderate	High
Parrott and Parrott	High	Moderate	Moderate
Stanley Trathen, and McCain	High	High	Moderate
Worthington	Moderate	High	High
Wright	High	High	High

While all theorists are either moderate or high in remediation and enrichment—as might be expected in theorists who are noted marital *counselors*—there is more divergence in prevention. Besides the selection bias (i.e., participants were selected foremost as therapists), such divergence may reflect an ambivalence in the field regarding premarital or neomarital counseling. Many have argued that it is often ineffective, or, at best, minimally effective, especially information-intensive programs (e.g., Worthington 1991). Others (e.g., the Parrotts and Stanley et al.) believe that prior to or early in marriage is the most important time in marriage. A paucity of research in the field leaves theorists to their personal hunches in determining the importance of prevention in marital counseling (see Markman and Hahlweg 1988 for a review).

Inclusion of Non-Christians or Not?

Of particular importance to many of the counselors is whether to counsel non-Christian couples, and if so, how? Although each counselor focuses primarily on Christian couples, most have also counseled non-Christian couples or couples in which only one partner is a Christian. Theorists suggested three approaches to nonbelieving clients:

(a) dropping Christian language and minimizing discussion of values, (b) informing the couple of the therapist's Christianity and discussing how it might affect counseling, and (c) meeting exclusively with couples who are comfortable working within a Christian value system.

Harley asserts that although his therapy is grounded in Christian beliefs, his approach is broadly applicable to all couples. His theory primarily uses secular concepts, and dropping the Christian language is uncomplicated or even unnecessary. Similarly, Guernsey directly applies his theory to non-Christian couples by removing Christian aspects. Stanley, Trathen, and McCain's approach, based on Markman's PREP (Prevention and Relationship Enhancement Program), is easily used in its original form for couples uncomfortable with a Christian framework. Oliver and Miller, using the Interpersonal Communication Programs model, can also easily use a secular version.

Worthington and Wright advocate informing the couple regarding the Christian values of the therapist. If couples continue to want counseling, Wright and Worthington generally work within their usual framework while de-emphasizing Christian metaphors and language.

More limited in application are the approaches of the Parrotts and Joy, for their models are designed specifically for couples who are comfortable operating within a Christian context.

The use of each of the three approaches to non-believing clients is directly related to the integration approaches of the individual therapists and to the flexibility of their programs. The more heavily therapists rely on Christian concepts, the less likely therapists are to meet with non-Christian couples or to reveal their Christian beliefs and values to their clients.

Duration of Therapy

Many theorists state that their therapy is geared toward brief time-limited interventions. This focus is often practically necessary, especially in organizations with limited funding, with pastors who have limited time, or in managed-care situations in which limits are imposed. Five of the approaches are conducted within a short-term format: Joy, approximately four sessions plus telephone follow-up;

Oliver and Miller, retreat setting or four group sessions; Parrott and Parrott, two-day workshop plus one year of mentoring, which consists of at least three meetings; Stanley, Trathen and McCain, short-term, often in workshop settings in churches or the community; and Worthington, typically assessment plus twelve sessions, or five sessions for pastoral counseling.

Other therapists do not limit the number of sessions with clients. They argue that as needs arise in therapy, the counselor is obligated to meet with a couple until the difficulty in their marriage is resolved, no matter how long it takes. Further exploration of the length of therapy will be addressed in the case-study portion of this chapter (see pp. 231–38).

How to Broaden the Audience

All of the theorists express the desire to see their theories extended to larger audiences and to achieve this by publishing books. Indeed, prior publication was one criterion for the selection of the theorists for participation in the present book. Some conduct empirical research (Oliver and Miller; the Parrotts; Stanley, Trathen, and McCain; Worthington) and some write conceptual articles in journals or popular magazines (Joy; the Parrotts; Stanley, Trathen, and McCain; Worthington; Wright). Harley and Stanley, Trathen, and McCain place particular importance on having their ideas presented to local churches and community organizations. Oliver and Miller, Harley, and Wright travel nationally to present information about their approach to various communities. Joy appears on nationally prominent television and radio programs. While some of these counselors may concentrate on their local practice, each is active in broadening his or her audience.

In the future, as technology affects counseling, we expect that additional broad applications of marital-counseling concepts will be available to couples. Couples may hook up to the Internet and converse immediately with staff at a mental-health center or attend therapy via virtual reality from the comfort of their own homes. While the younger generation of theorists may relish the many counseling possibilities available through technology, reflective therapists warn that technology can be misused and cause trouble for couples already heading in a destructive direction. The warmth and expertise of a human therapist cannot be replaced by computers or technology. It is important that checks and balances exist to maximize the likelihood that positive outcomes are the result of new methods of intervention.

Question 3
What are your foci for counseling?

Is the counselor, the clients as individuals, or the clients as a couple the focus of therapy? Will therapy focus on all of the clients' relationships (e.g., with parents, siblings, children, and grand-children), or will it focus only on the partners' relationship with each other? The focus is heavily influenced by each theorist's style and approach. Moreover, the success of both those who focus on individuals and those who focus on couples leads us to conclude that no matter where the intervention may focus, positive change can occur.

Determining who the client is in marital therapy depends on the counselor's theory. Wright tends to work with either couples or individuals. However, even in couples therapy, he still strives for individual changes. Joy's technique of private documentation of experiences reveals his emphasis on improving individuals. The Parrotts point to a paradox that relationship change requires individuals to change. Worthington prefers to work with both partners together at improving their relationship. Although sometimes individuals come for counseling, Worthington still works with them to improve their marriage. Oliver and Miller; Stanley, Trathan, and McCain; and the Parrotts work with couples almost exclusively.

Modeling Interpersonal Relations

Several theorists stress the importance of their modeling good interpersonal relations; for example, the Parrotts view this as a key to aiding the couple. Such modeling is especially applicable in their therapy because they conjointly meet with each couple. Every session of the foursome allows the husband-wife therapy team to model good relating styles. Wright also believes that modeling appropriate relating styles is essential to enabling a couple to be more fulfilled in their marriage. He tries to model good communication with each partner. In addition, Oliver and Miller, in the Interpersonal Communication Programs, show videotapes of models who demonstrate good and poor communication.

Personal History

Three counselors, influenced by psychodynamic theories, focus heavily on each partner's personal history albeit different aspects of that history. Relying on the parent-child bond to explain "the center of the human dilemma," Guernsey believes that relational patterns are the most important part of therapy. Exploring generational stories is important to Joy and the Parrotts. The Parrotts also explore the history of their clients' sibling relationships as well as parental relationships to uncover the couple's relational style. They broaden their perspective further to include all early relationships to gain a vivid picture of the couple's social history. Joy investigates the couple's history prior to the partners' meeting and marrying, for he believes that urging partners to document their personal histories will produce insight and stimulate emotional unloading.

Spiritual Intimacy

How much do Christian counselors focus on enhancing a couple's relationship with God? Two approaches mention the couple's relationship with God and the therapist's role in discipling. Oliver and Miller report testimonies that their skills-training program has helped people put their faith into practice. Worthington believes that the counselor is discipled by God and others and then, in turn, disciples clients. Although other counselors did not specifically mention a discipling relationship in response to Question 3, all accentuated their belief in the importance of an intimate relationship with God.

Question 4
How is your marriage counseling conducted?

Assessment

Of practical significance to all therapists is gaining an understanding of the variety of assessments that are useful in therapy. Therapists in six of the eight approaches advocate using a formal assessment instrument. Others might argue that assessment instruments detract from the role of the therapist by "pigeon-holing" couples. These therapists rely more heavily on the interview to evaluate couples entering therapy.

Those advocating the use of assessment instruments reveal that numerous ones are available to Christian marriage counselors. Both standardized instruments and theorist-created ones (indicated by *) were recommended.

Joy—Myers-Briggs Type Indicator (MBTI)

Harley—Minnesota Multiphasic Personality Inventory (MMPI), *Personal History Questionnaire, *Emotional Needs Questionnaire, *Love Busters Questionnaire, *Love Bank Inventory

Oliver and Miller—*skills assessment, *prequestionnaire, *workbook to assess communication skills

Parrott and Parrott—genogram interview, FACES III

Worthington—Couple's Precounseling Inventory (CPCI), Personal Assessment of Intimacy in Relationships (PAIR)

Wright—*Marital Assessment Inventory (MAI), MBTI

The standardized and theorist-created instruments both have benefits. Standardized ones are viewed as a useful and efficient way to measure couples' needs, and these measures help counselors determine which couples may need referrals to individual therapy, physicians, or other counselors. Moreover, standardized assessments have norms to aid therapists in interpreting the data. (For other examples of assessment instruments, see Filsinger 1983 and

Fredman and Sherman 1987.) Many therapists have developed their own instruments to assess marriages; these tools direct the partners' attention where the counselors want it.

Homework

Marital counselors must decide whether to include homework, and if so, how. Therapists disagree as to where the most powerful work of therapy is done—in session or in homework. A clue to each therapist's view is found in the emphasis, or lack of emphasis, each places on work the clients are to do at home (see table 3).

The variety of homework assignments reveals the creativity of Christian counselors. The counselor's theory, personal preference, and compatibility with individuals' needs help to determine which homework assignments are given. Theorists who are influenced by cognitive-behavioral therapy encourage skill building and outside reading; those who value modeling encourage the use of audiovisual material.

Table 3

Homework

Type	Theorists Who Advocate Use
reading/ workbook tasks	Harley; Oliver and Miller; Stanley, Trathen, and McCain; Wright
skills and activities	Harley (romantic); Oliver and Miller (skill mats); Stanley, Trathen, and McCain (Ground Rules); Worthington (forgiveness)
audiovisual materials	Stanley, Trathen, and McCain; Wright
journal writing/ documentation	Joy; Parrott and Parrott
prayer/ Scripture reading	Oliver and Miller; Stanley, Trathen, and McCain

The influence of psychodynamic and historical theories on Joy and the Parrotts is revealed in their assignment of journal writing.

Of the eight approaches, only two (Oliver and Miller; Stanley, Trathen, and McCain) explicitly assign prayer and Scripture reading for a couple's homework, though presumably all would agree that both prayer and Scripture reading would help most marriages. Pastoral counselors might challenge other Christian marital counselors to utilize more explicitly the positive influence of ecclesiastically derived activities and of the Holy Spirit. If there is some agreement, which there appears to be, that a main problem in all marriages is sin, then pastors might challenge those theorists who fail to address spirituality when attempting to solve marital problems.

Question 5
How do you deal with a few of the common marital problems?

All counselors seem to agree on one thing—marriage problems originate in people's sinful nature. However, there is no agreement as to how that sinful nature is manifested. Exactly how do marriages break down? What difficulties lead to distressing marriages and perhaps divorce? The theorists suggest ways to handle six common marital problems: gender differences, intimacy, conflict, unmet needs, affairs, and divorce. How to handle each problem creates some stark choices for marital therapists.

Gender Differences

Men and women have been raised with different expectations of their own marriage roles, expectations of their spouse, and ways of interacting with others. Harley, Joy, Oliver and Miller, Wright, and the Parrotts believe that gender difficulties are a common problem in marriages. Through two examples of persons coping with gender problems, Joy emphasizes auditing family history and the pair-bonding sequence to deal with gender problems. Oliver and Miller especially emphasize communication needs that arise from gender differences. The other theorists believe that gender differences can be handled by educating the couple on some common differences in the needs of males and females.

Intimacy

The Parrotts advocate treating intimacy problems by encouraging couples to build outside relationships to handle enmeshment. In contrast, Worthington addresses intimacy by encouraging couples to modify their schedules so they spend more time together (if they currently feel they spend too little time together). He also suggests that partners focus on valuing each other. Harley's theory is built on increasing romantic love. Joy's theory focuses on sexual intimacy. Theorists help couples build intimacy in various ways. Is romance the key, as Harley says, or sexual intimacy, as Joy suggests, or valuing love, as Worthington suggests? Is it more important to give each person personal space, as the Parrotts say, or to spend more time together, as Worthington suggests?

These various approaches lead to deeper questions concerning intimacy: Can intimacy be built by behaving more pleasantly? Is intimacy a reciprocal exchange process? Or is it a mandate for each partner to pursue regardless of what the other partner does? Is intimacy some deep mystical bonding that is not dependent on one's partner? Or is it a product of simply behaving intimately or spending time together? Addressing these questions should be a part of formulating one's own marital-counseling theory and practice.

Conflict

Probably the most universal problem presented in marital counseling is conflict between partners. Each of the five approaches that addressed conflicts advocate the use of some form of communication training to resolve them. The Parrotts encourage couples to state their feelings and use a Conflict Card to facilitate equal communication for both partners. Oliver and Miller encourage couples to use an approach to communication in which partners step on various parts of an Awareness Wheel mat or a responding mat and "map" conflicts. Stanley, Trathen, and McCain encourage couples to use Ground Rules and to pass "the floor" to help them communicate better. Wright directs couples to investigate new approaches to handle conflict as well as to empathize with each other. More specifically, he encourages partners to write an angry letter, which will never be sent, to address some of the conflict. Worthington educates the couple to be aware of the intent versus the impact of statements that provoke each partner, and he helps couples identify the interests behind the positions partners stake out (Fisher & Ury 1983).

Questions regarding conflict still remain: Is conflict resolution the goal of marital therapy? Does a low level of conflict between partners necessarily indicate a fulfilled marriage? Is there a positive purpose to conflict in marriage? Is there a connection between conflict and sin? We have noted those therapists who advocate communication as the key to resolving differences. Others might believe that conflicts can be resolved by building intimacy, meeting deep needs, or understanding gender differences. Some therapists may even encourage *increased* conflict, but focus on how it is managed.

Unmet Needs

Should an individual's unmet needs be met through one's spouse or through other aspects of one's life, such as job, children, leisure activities, or friends? What is the importance of God in meeting needs? Crabb (1982, 1991) has argued persuasively that a partner can *never* meet one's needs totally; thus, partners must look to God—not to each other—to meet their needs.

Harley, Wright, and Oliver and Miller specifically identify unmet needs as a common presenting problem. Harley's marriage-enrichment seminars encourage partners to look for ways to meet each other's needs. He affirms that this will create deeper and more caring relationships. Wright advocates cherishing days as a way couples can meet each other's needs, with the hope that cherishing will become natural for the couple. In Oliver and Miller's communication model, spouses communicate their needs in session.

The approaches of Harley, Wright, and Oliver and Miller focus on each individual's doing all that he or she can to meet the partner's needs. What happens when partners cannot or will not meet each other's needs? How does the concept of marriage as a covenant, which was popular with several theorists, fit into the discussion? If partners covenant to serve one another, how should it relate to need fulfillment? These questions remain unanswered, revealing an issue that is particularly underdeveloped in the field of marital theory and counseling.

Affairs

Several therapeutic approaches propose ways to handle affairs. Wright helps the couple symbolically and literally expel the third party from the marriage. Stanley, Trathen, and McCain, through Christian PREP, encourage the couple to gain a deeper understanding of their commitment for each other. In marked contrast, Guernsey's psychodynamic approach delves into the partners' narcissistic injuries while encouraging forgiveness. Which is more important—rebuilding the marriage toward the future or focusing on the reasons why the affair occurred? Or both? The lines are drawn according to theory, with psychodynamic theorists focusing on understanding the past and cognitive-behavioral and solution-oriented theorists focusing on changing the future.

Divorce

Should a Christian counselor discourage and/or encourage divorce? Three counselors—Guernsey, Harley, Wright—specifically addressed how to handle a couple in the midst of divorce. Guernsey, consistent with his psychodynamic stance, takes the most impartial perspective, acknowledging each couple's responsibility in deciding whether the marriage can be resurrected. Conversely, Wright encourages couples to contract for three months of commitment and therapy before initiating divorce. His approach consists of bibliotherapy, contracts with partners to be amicable with one another, and agreements to attend a workshop for divorce recoverers. He believes that through such activities the partners get a good idea of what divorce will mean for them. Harley encourages couples contemplating divorce to participate in his Love Busters program in an attempt to preserve the marriage.

Task 1

Respond to the case study by telling precisely how you might typically treat it, in how many sessions, in what order, and with what responses by the clients throughout counseling. One restriction: Assume that between the third and fourth counseling sessions with you—regardless of what had gone on during the previous session—the couple had a major argument and come to the fourth session in some crisis.

Task 2

Create a dialogue between the counselor and the couple (or one spouse, if you prefer) showing how you might deal with communication difficulties.

The case of Art and Pam presents a unique opportunity to evaluate how counselors might work with a particular couple in coping with marital problems. It is especially interesting to note which problem counselors chose to address and how they proposed to deal with it. Other topics of interest arising from the responses to Tasks 1 and 2 are outcome expectancies, the various ways therapists begin therapy, and their styles of relating to couples.

The case of Art and Pam was completely fictitious, as were all of the simulated dialogues. As such, the responses to the case study represent how theorists *describe* their counseling more than how

Table 4

Issues Addressed by Theorists in the Case of Art and Pam

Therapist(s)	Guernsey	Harley	Joy	Oliver and Miller	Parrott and Parrott	Stanley, Trathen, and McCain	Worthington	Wright
Issue								
Need fulfillment	not	con	not	not	not	not	min	not
New habits, patterns, or skills	mod	mod	mod	con	min	mod	con	con
Past and/or family of origin	con	not	con	not	con	mod	min	mod
Forgiveness	not	not	not	min	mod	mod	mod	not
Intimacy	mod	not	not	not	mod	not	mod	not
Cultural differences	not	not	not	not	mod	not	not	not
Affair	min	not	min	not	mod	min	mod	min
Gender differences	not	mod	not	not	not	min	not	mod
Conflict resolution	mod	mod	mod	mod	not	con	mod	mod
Infertility	not	not	min	mod	mod	min	not	not
Spiritual intimacy	min	not	not	mod	not	min	min	mod
Career	not	not	not	min	mod	not	not	not

Note: con = concentration of therapy
mod = addressed to a moderate degree
min = minimally addressed
not = not directly addressed

they actually counsel. Notably missing are the surprises that clients drop on their counselors—both the moment-by-moment surprise of conversation and the weekly or monthly unexpected twists and turns of real life. Nonetheless, the theorists' descriptions of how they might treat Art and Pam give a different perspective on their counseling than does mere explications of theory (see table 4 for a summary of issues addressed by the theorists).

Beginning Therapy

Whenever any couple enters into therapy with a counselor, a series of decisions must be made regarding what problems will be addressed and in what order. The first decision therapists must make is how to begin therapy. Some begin with formal assessments that last from one to two sessions (Joy; Harley; Oliver and Miller; Worthington) because, they argue, a complete understanding of the couple and their problem is necessary before progressing. Beneficial effects can, indeed, stem from assessment, which might account for as much as one-third of the gains achieved in marriage enrichment (Worthington et al. 1995). Engaging the couple in change from the start, other therapists weave assessment and therapy together (Stanley, Trathen, and McCain; Wright) because they view beginning therapy as necessary from the first session onward to meet the immediate needs of the couple.

Identifying and Addressing Problems

Pam and Art's inability to resolve their conflicts was their presenting problem, which the therapists approached in several ways. Short-term or solution-oriented theorists (Oliver and Miller; Stanley, Trathen, and McCain; Worthington; Wright) addressed the presenting problem as central to therapy. Harley and the Parrotts saw conflict as a by-product of an unhappy relationship and thus did not address conflict as the direct cause of the problem. Guernsey encouraged conflict in the couple since he views conflict as a sign of growth.

Which one of Art and Pam's problems did therapists focus on primarily? The counselors took several paths. Most worked on developing new skills in communication and interpersonal relations (Oliver and Miller; Stanley, Trathen, and McCain; Worthington; Wright). Harley stressed mutual need fulfillment as primary. Others focused on the past, believing that in order to help change the couple's future they as therapists must first understand Art and Pam's past (Guernsey; Joy; Parrott and Parrott). It appears that the primary focus is determined by the therapists' psychological theory. Psychodynamic theorists focused on the past. Solution-oriented and cognitive-behavioral theorists challenged the couple to build new skills. Harley's theory led him to focus on the fulfillment of needs.

The therapists also addressed a variety of secondary problems experienced by Art and Pam.

Gender differences. Harley, Stanley, Trathen, and McCain, and Wright specifically addressed gender differences. Each therapist's intent was that Art and Pam would understand each other and appreciate their gender differences.

Resolving differences. Most therapists attempted to help Art and Pam resolve their differences. Guernsey, influenced by psychodynamic theory, sees conflict as a sign of growth in the couple. Joy views conflict as a catastrophe, much like a death, and so encourages couples to grieve over the losses of their marriages. By having couples focus on their grief, Joy believes they will find a common goal in overcoming their marital difficulties.

Oliver and Miller and the Parrotts addressed Pam's concerns about her career and the couple's infertility. They approached both problems sensitively while encouraging conflict resolution regarding the topics and helping the couple plan for the future.

Only the Parrotts addressed Art and Pam's cultural differences. As the influence of culture becomes more prominent in psychology, it will be interesting to see whether culture will play a larger part in Christian marital counseling.

Intimacy. Only Wright directly addressed the topic of intimacy with Art and Pam. Indeed, he emphasized intimacy building and incorporated spiritual intimacy as well. Perhaps other counselors saw spiritual intimacy as an advanced marriage-enrichment topic for which Art and Pam were not yet ready. However, some of the counselors tried to help Art and Pam build intimacy albeit in a variety of ways.

Affair. Each counselor who dealt with Art's affair did so in conjunction with forgiveness and sexual fulfillment. Guernsey worked with Art and Pam's sex life. Wright offered questions for probing how "forgiven" Art's affair really was. The Parrotts sought confession and forgiveness, while framing the cause of the affair into a systemic framework. Worthington addressed the affair, working toward forgiveness.

Table 5

Analysis of Each Therapist's Fictional Dialogue with Art and Pam

	Harley	Joy	Oliver and Miller	Parrott and Parrott (Les)	(Leslie)	Stanley, Trathen, and McCain	Worthington	Wright
Number of words (percent)								
Therapist	262	801	163	182	223	276	649	503
	(43%)	(56%)	(27%)	(16%)	(20%)	(35%)	(70%)	(41%)
Art	348	620	278	410		273	110	530
	(57%)	(44%)	(46%)	(36%)		(35%)	(13%)	(46%)
Pam	0	0	166	310		236	146	181
	(0%)	(0%)	(27%)	(28%)		(30%)	(17%)	(15%)
Number of Statements								
Therapist	13	19	13	13	14	12	22	23
Art	14	18	15	20		13	10	19
Pam	0	0	12	12		11	1	3
Mean Words Per Statement								
Therapist	0.0	21.9	12.5	13.8	15.9	23.0	29.0	21.9
Art	24.9	34.4	18.5	20.5		21.0	11.0	27.9
Pam	0.0	0.0	13.8	25.8		21.4	12.2	60.3

Dialogue Styles

The amount of simulated dialogue between the therapists and the couple is too small for any examination to lead to definite conclusions. However, a simple evaluation of the number of statements, words, words per statement, and the types of statements in the fictitious dialogues suggests trends in the way counselors conduct their therapy.

Note, however, that examining word counts and types of statements can be misleading. You are encouraged to read each of the dialogues in a single sitting and form overall impressions and then to compare your impressions of the dialogues with the objective indices.

Two styles of counseling are evident from the dialogues—the therapist as coach and the therapist as individual counselor. Taking on the role of director as the couple interacted in session, the therapist as coach talked about a third to a half as often as Art and Pam (Oliver and Miller; Stanley, Trathen, and McCain). Counseling couples much as they would individuals, other therapists roughly divided their time equally between themselves and each spouse. These therapists tended to have conversations with first one spouse and then with the other, talking about equally with Art and Pam (Harley; Joy; Parrott and Parrot; Wright).

Analyzing the directive, reflective, and interpretive statements of the therapists reveals that they tended to be rather directive, to reflect seldom, and to vary widely in their use of interpretation. Directive statements are sentences or phrases that focus or redirect therapy (e.g., "Now I would like you to . . ." or "Would you do that?"). Reflective statements paraphrase content or label the feelings of the client. Interpretive statements reframe the client's words into the therapist's theoretical terminology.

Table 6

Summary of Types of Statements Made by Therapists

	Directive Statements	Interpretive Statements	Reflective Statements
Harley	10	3	0
Joy	9	9	0
Oliver and Miller	10	1	0
Parrott and Parrott:			
Les	10	4	0
Leslie	6	5	1
Stanley, Trathen, and McCain	10	2	0
Worthington	11	9	1
Wright	15	7	3

Most of the therapists were directive in 50 to 75 percent of their statements, which is quite different from individual therapy. While they often blended other types of statements along with the directive, they clearly were working in therapy toward a goal. This is best exhibited in Stanley, Trathen, and McCain's highly directive dialogue in which they repeatedly encouraged partners to engage in their suggested therapeutic activities. The therapists acted as a "traffic cop" to direct the couple toward playing by the Speaker/Listener rules and sharing their feelings with one another. Joy was less directive in his interaction in an individual session with Art. Only about half of Joy's statements had a directive component to them, and he was as likely to give an interpretive statement as to be directive. None of the counselors reflected the clients' feelings or content often. All were more likely to direct the session or interpret the clients' statements.

Although tables 5 and 6 suggest differences in therapeutic styles of interaction with couples, we clearly do not have large enough samples of dialogue to make any conclusions about each therapist's definitive style. Each counselor is proficient in his or her field and is flexible in dealing with real clients. However, the differences in style suggest other decisions that Christian marital counselors must make. Will you speak as often as clients, less often, or more? How directive, reflective, and interpretive will you be? What will your style of interaction be? How often will you change your focus from one partner to the other? Will you promote conversation between partners or direct the conversation? Your theory, personal style, and specific goals for therapy will substantially determine your interaction style.

Outcome

How did theorists expect Art and Pam's marriage to turn out after therapy? Most of the counselors projected a positive ending with the couple still together in an improved marriage. Joy did not state a predicted outcome. Despite broad agreement regarding the outcome, the therapists varied widely regarding the number of sessions necessary to reach it. Oliver and Miller projected meeting with the couple the fewest times—only six. At the other extreme, the Parrotts and Guernsey expected that three to six months of weekly sessions would be needed. Their Bowenian and psychoanalytic orientations, respectively, lengthen their expectations of therapy. Harley predicted ten sessions; Worthington, eight; and Stanley, Trathen, and McCain, fifteen. Each of these uses a version of the cognitive-behavioral and short-term therapy model.

Marriage counseling is moving toward shorter models of therapy, with many recent theorists proposing fewer than ten sessions. Shorter to moderate lengths of therapy are influenced by a variety of factors including theory, client expectations, financial considerations, managed-care and insurance limitations, and counselor/pastor availability. The goals of brief therapy are to give the couple the basic skills to improve their marriage, to point the couple in the right direction, and to have the couple work to improve the marriage primarily outside of therapy.

The debate over the optimal length of therapy rages. Some argue that brief therapy is not simply an unpleasant reality foisted upon unwilling therapists by hostile, greedy authorities concerned only about the cost of treatment. Rather, they argue that brief solution-focused therapy is desirable for therapist *and patient* needs. Others argue that a therapist is doing a disservice to a couple if treatment ends after only a few sessions. They believe that short-term therapy is like doing emergency-room treatment that provides short-term "fixes," but does not offer real solutions.

Conclusion

Obviously, this text cannot exhaustively address all styles of Christian marital counseling. There are many talented, articulate theorists writing about Christian marriage counseling other than those appearing in this volume. Unfortunately, not every theorist could fit. Yet, this text offers us material to be critically evaluated and experimented with in our own practices, theories, and research.

The question with which we began still remains: What is Christian about Christian marital therapy? The integration of Christianity and marital counseling is still in its childhood. While many therapists refer to Scripture and Christian concepts in theory, the therapists' limited application of them in practice is likely to leave many Christian couples wanting. This is especially true in the areas of homework, spiritual growth, and the integration of theories. What makes Christian marital counseling unique is its emphasis on Christian values and beliefs. These values and beliefs must be the foundation of theory and practice if Christian marital therapists are to find their own place in the couples therapy field.

As new practitioners enter the field of Christian marital counseling, a barrage of questions face them: What kinds of clients will I see? What will I focus on in my sessions? How will I integrate faith into practice? What will be my interaction style? No one technique or style of Christian marital counseling has arisen as *the* leading Christian style. Perhaps that is God's plan. Each approach is an experiment in helping Christian marriages. Perhaps God desires for us to find the answers to the questions with hard work, experimentation (formal and informal), and reliance on the Holy Spirit. We hope this text has offered novice and experienced practitioners ideas to explore as they seek to improve their personal approach. We also hope it has sparked new ideas for researchers.

This chapter reveals many of the controversies considered in the prevalent positions of theory, style, goals, conceptualizations, and integration in Christian marital counseling. The maze seems daunting at first, but as we become oriented it is exciting to explore the tunnels and avenues of the Christian marital-counseling field. We hope we have helped you continue to find your own way.

References

Beitman, B. D., M. R. Goldfried, and J. C. Norcross. 1989. The movement toward integrating the psychotherapies: An overview. *American Journal of Psychiatry* 146:138–47.

Crabb, L. J., Jr. 1982. *The marriage builder*. Grand Rapids: Zondervan.

———. 1991. *Men and women: Enjoying the difference*. Grand Rapids: Zondervan.

deShazer, S. 1988. *Clues: Investigating solutions in brief therapy*. New York: Norton.

Filsinger, E. E., ed. 1983. *Marriage and family assessment: A sourcebook for family therapy*. Beverly Hills, Calif.: Sage Publications.

Fisher, R., and W. Ury. 1983. *Getting to yes: Negotiating agreement without giving in*. Middlesex, U. K.: Penguin.

Fredman, N., and R. Sherman. 1987. *Handbook of measurements for marriage and family therapy*. New York: Brunner/Mazel.

Markman, H. J., and K. Hahlweg. 1988. Effectiveness of behavioral marital therapy: Empirical status of behavioral techniques in preventing and alleviating marital distress. *Journal of Consulting and Clinical Psychology* 56:440–47.

Norcross, J. C., ed. 1993. Research directions for psychotherapy integration: A roundtable. *Journal of Psychotherapy Integration* 3:91–131.

Worthington, E. L., Jr. 1989. *Marriage counseling: A Christian approach to counseling couples*. Downers Grove, Ill.: InterVarsity.

———. 1991. *Counseling before marriage*. Dallas: Word Books.

Worthington, E. L., Jr., M. E. McCullough, J. L.Shortz, E. J. Mindes, S. J. Sandage, and J. M. Chartrand. 1995. Can couples assessment and feedback improve relationships? Assessment as a brief relationship-enrichment procedure. *Journal of Counseling Psychology* 42:466–75.

Wright, H. N. 1981. *Marital counseling: A biblical, behavioral, cognitive approach*. San Francisco: Harper and Row.

Index